CAMEROON'S PUBLIC SERVICE LAW

Droits africains et malgache

Collection dirigée par Magloire ONDOA

La collection « Droits africains et malgache » accueille les travaux de chercheurs, enseignants et étudiants, ou praticiens, soucieux de contribuer à cette œuvre de réconciliation du droit en vigueur avec le droit étudié, d'une part ; de l'autre, d'élimination de la distance séparant les citoyens africains de leurs droits vivants, c'est-à-dire, ceux qui leur sont effectivement appliqués.

Déjà parus

Jacques BIAKAN, *Droit des marchés publics au Cameroun. Contribution à l'étude des contrats publics*, 2011.
Jean GATSI, *Le droit OHADA des sociétés coopératives*, 2011.
Gustave NGUEDA NDIEFOUO, *La douane camerounaise à l'ère de la facilitation des échanges commerciaux*, 2011.
Joseph OWONA, *Le contentieux administratif de la République du Cameroun*, 2011.
Joseph OWONA, *La décentralisation camerounaise*, 2011.
Joseph OWONA, *Droit de la fonction publique camerounaise*, 2011.
Anicet ABAN ATANGANA, *Administration fiscale et contribuable au Cameroun*, 2010.

Joseph Owona

CAMEROON'S PUBLIC SERVICE LAW

L'Harmattan

FROM THE AUTHOR

Joseph OWONA et **NJOH MOUELLE Ebénézer,** *Encyclopédie de la République Unie du Cameroun* (4 tomes), Nouvelles Éditions Africaines, Dakar Abidjan, 1981.

Joseph OWONA et **SIKHE Camara,** sous-direction PF GONIDEC.

Encyclopédie Juridique de l'Afrique, Tome II, Droit International et Relations Internationales, Nouvelles Éditions Africaines, Dakar Abidjan, 1982.

Joseph OWONA, *Droit constitutionnel et Régimes politiques africains,* Manuels B.L. 3, Mondes en devenir, Berger Levrault, Paris, Mars 1985.

Joseph OWONA, *La Nouvelle voie chinoise ou l'air pur du soir,* Mondes en devenir XXIX, Points chauds 14, Berger Levrault, Paris, Mars 1986.

Joseph OWONA, *La République populaire démocratique de Corée,* Mondes en devenir LIV, Points chauds 14, Berger Levrault, Paris, Mars 1987.

Joseph OWONA, *Droit Administratif spécial de la République du Cameroun,* EDICEF, Série Manuels et Travaux de l'Université de Yaoundé, 1985.

Joseph OWONA, *Aperçu sur les principes élémentaires du Droit International contemporain,* Travaux de recherches de l'Université de Yaoundé, 1986.

Joseph OWONA, *Droits constitutionnels et institutions politiques du monde contemporain : étude comparative*, L'Harmattan, Paris, Septembre 2010.

5-7, rue de l'Ecole-Polytechnique, 75005 Paris

http://www.librairieharmattan.com
diffusion.harmattan@wanadoo.fr
harmattan1@wanadoo.fr

ISBN : 978-2-296-96469-3
EAN : 9782296964693

ACKNOWLEDGMENTS

I would like to address my special thanks to a generation of shadow workers whose typing, revision and formatting helped shape up the present work in its didactic core. I think most especially of **Sylvestre GWET MATIP**, an environmentalist, fundamentalist of biology, and **Berthine NSEOUGMOE**, of the J.O International consulting firm.

GENERAL INTRODUCTION

I. CONCEPT OF THE PUBLIC SERVICE

What is the public service ?

This recent notion that was barely in use thirty (30) years [1] ago may carry at least three different meanings :

I.1- Fundamental meaning

The term "public service" ordinarily designates all staff, that is to say, all the people working for the State, and in some cases and conditions[2], for decentralized local authorities.

The regulatory provisions are eloquently clear to this effect :

"The public service of the State is constituted by all the work positions corresponding to different levels of classification. It is organized in corps, income brackets, ranks and categories".

"Local governments freely recruit and manage the necessary personnel to accomplish their tasks in accordance with the laws and regulations and the status of the staff in question is determined by presidential decree."

"These provisions, in addition to the public service of the State, allow for the existence of the new decentralized regional and local authorities, which are yet to be set up. There are therefore state civil servants and local government civil servants.

However, it should be noted that "*civil servants and staff made available (on secondment) to local authorities continue to be governed by the* ***general rules and regulations*** *and the* ***labour code***".

The organic meaning can thus be summarized in these terms :

---

[1] GAZIER (F.), *La fonction publique dans le monde*, Edition Cujas. P13.
TEKAM (G.J.), *Fonction publique camerounaise, Statut général et textes d'application – Recueil des textes commentés,* 311 pages, secrétariat général des services du Premier ministre.

[2] Refer to article 19 of law n° 2004-17 of july 22 on the orientation of the decentralization.

- a State public service governed by the general rules and regulations ;

- and a parallel civil service, to be created in the context of decentralization, governed by a Presidential decree,

- state employees governed under the labour code and recruited by decision, that is to say a unilateral act of the administration (from category 6 to category 12), are no longer considered as civil servants[1].

I.2- Formal meaning

From a formal point of view, the civil service refers to a legal regime applicable to a class of public officials.

"*The civil servant is a person possessing a permanent status within the hierarchy of the State administration*".

The civil servant, vis-à-vis the administration, is in a "*statutory and regulatory situation*" whereas state agents are governed by the labour code, thus, from an essential legal regime of the common social law, they are not civil servants and their relationship with the administration is contractual.

I.3- Material meaning

Finally, the public service may simply mean the permanent participation, in a professional capacity, in the actions of the public legal entities of the State and decentralized communities.

"*Shall be considered a civil servant any person holding a permanent job*" within the set-up of the hierarchy of government departments[2].

Provision must be made for the job position in the State budget. It corresponds to all the tasks, duties and responsibilities requiring special knowledge and skills. A change of job position is allowed on condition that this position corresponds to some special knowledge and skills.

A corps is made up of all the civil servants carrying out specific duties within a given sector of activity and governed by the same regulations.

The cadre includes all the positions reserved for staff recruited at the same level of education or professional qualification. They are subject to the same treatment.

---

[1] Refer to TEKAM, *Fonction publique camerounaise, Op cit.,* p. 7.

[2] Refer to article 3 of the general rules and regulations of the public service.

The rank defines the position of the civil servant in the hierarchy of his income bracket.

The "*public service*" therefore refers to so many things : all civil servants of the State and decentralized communities to which must be added State agents or contract workers, the public law legal regime applicable to them or the hierarchy of corps holding permanent job positions within the State.

II. STATE PERSONNEL IN CAMEROON : Data and Evolution

The development of administrative staff has known considerable growth in Cameroon. Three major periods mark this evolution, first from colonization to independence, then the period under structural adjustment, and the present time.

II.1- THE SETTING UP A PUBLIC SERVICE IN CAMEROON : from the colonial era to 1982

The german colonizers emphasized the training of cameroonians to actively assist them. By 1913, there existed several specialized schools notably the schools of nursing in Buea and Victoria, the first school of agriculture in the country opened in 1910. At the beginning of French colonization, the indigenous staff, as valuable assistants to the colonial administration and private enterprises, was trained at the senior primary school in Yaoundé in a three-year course that prepared for careers as education instructors, central service officials, postal workers, nurses and agricultural instructors. The teacher training college at Foulassi, the minor seminary at Akono and two mission schools played a similar[1] role.

Two acts of the French commissioner in Cameroon as from 1921 organized local European staff as well as local native staff in Cameroon[2].

This embryonic colonial civil service was to experience rapid growth with the country's accession to autonomy and independence. Official statistics as of june 30, 1974 show 13,494 State employees for the former Eastern Cameroon alone and 17,154 employees for the entire Republic. By march 31st, 1976, these figures had risen to 36,659. And as at 31

[1] Refer to YOUBI (J. F.), « La Camerounisation des cadres », Mémoire de licence en droit, Faculté de Droit et des Sciences économiques, UY, 1974, pp.11-12.
[2] Ibid.

december 1982, the cameroonian public service had 40,200 tenured civil servants (table 1) and 7,704 contract employees (table 1).

Table 1 : Evolution of Cameroonian State employees by category and year of enrolment from 1962 to 1982

Nos	Year	Number of civil servants per category							Absolute Increment	Rate %
		A2	A1	B2	B1	C	D	TOTAL		
1	1962	76	185	_	571	2 510	3 624	6 966	717	11,47
2	1963	104	195	9	747	2 713	3 884	7 652	686	9,85
3	1964	104	303	11	984	2 814	3 986	8 206	554	7,24
4	1965	155	351	17	1 12	3 050	4 089	8 774	568	6,92
5	1966	223	415	83	1 277	3 311	4 621	9 929	1 155	13,16
6	1967	259	487	113	1 552	3 581	5 106	11 098	1 169	1177
7	1968	270	573	141	1 672	3 863	5 402	11 921	823	7,42
8	1969	298	741	159	1 808	3 402*	4 875*	11 283*	-638	-5,35
9	1970	559	913	76	1 968	3 620	4 325*	11 461*	178	1,58
10	1971	568	1 041	88	2 261	3 800	4 655	12 412	952	8,31
11	1972	667	1 110	149	2 445	3 920	5 203	13 494	1 081	8,71
12	1973	783	1 362	209	3 029	4 736	6 091	16 210**	2 716	20,13
13	1974	801	1 381	298	3 574	5 351	6 696	18 101**	1 891	11,67
14	1975	855	1 417	385	3 977	6 124	6 914	19 672	1 517	8,68
15	1976	981	1 701	409	4 204	7 258	7 789	22 342	2 670	13,57
16	1977	1 163	2 009	453	4 530	8 047	8 008	24 193	1 851	8,2
17	1978	1 343	2 311	569	5 200	9 669	8 308	27 400	3 207	13,26
18	1979	1 452	2 432	726	5 576	10 770	9 108	30 064	2 664	9,72
19	1980	1 665	2 783	875	6 222	12 187	9 659	33 391	3 327	11,07
20	1981	2 030	3 249	1 024	6 949	13 324	10 343	36 919	3 528	10,56
21	1982	2 398	3 604	1 182	7 943	14 403	10 670	40 200	3 281	8,89

Source : Public Service. Workforce Control Department, Bureau of Statistics.

*Except for the personnel of the Police corps that became autonomous. That explains the drastic fall in numbers of State employees down to a -5.5% rate.

** Including State employees of the former Western Cameroon, taken into account after the merger of the three public services. Hence the jump from 8,71% to 20,13%.

We notice that in 1982 the education sector employed 15,446 persons, thus 38,42% of the state agents, ahead of the technical sector (21,25%), medical and social sector (17,13%), administrative and law sectors (16,86%)...

Table 2 : Number of State employees per sector of activities (1981-1982)

Rank : Sector	Total number as of Dec. 31, 1981	Total number as of Dec. 31, 1982	Absolute increment	Rate in %	Percentage compared to the whole
1st : Education	14 146	15 446	1 300	9,19	38,42
2nd : Technical	7 863	8 543	680	8,65	21,25
3rd : Medical	6 326	6 887	561	8,87	17,13
4th : Administration And Law	6 133	6 775	642	10,47	16,86
5th : Finance	2 451	2 549	98	4,00	6,34
Total	36 919	40 200	3 281	8,89	100,00

Source : Public Service. Workforce Control Department. Bureau of Statistics.

II.2- WORKFORCE DEVELOPMENT : from structural adjustment to nowadays (1982 – 2008)

The steady increase in the number of civil servants in all categories still remains a constant trend. However, the economic crisis of the 80s followed by a necessary structural adjustment of the workforce in 1990 hence led thereof to a remarkable reduction.

From 1990 to 1994, the number of civil servants was modest. It dropped (from 74,018 to 71,699), but the difference was offset by the use of workers recruited on decision and contract basis. In effect, during this period, the number of workers progressively move from 5921 up to 6375 for contract workers and from 15 544 up to 16 735 for workers recruited on the decisional basis (see table 2).

The year 1998 represents a significant milestone in the reduction of State employees workforce with a total of 83,788, which was lower than the 1990 total of 95,483. This represents a reduction of about 12,000 workers, with 4,294 being civil servants and 6,282 workers recruited on decisional basis.

The upward trend resumed in 1999 when the global number shot up to over 100,000 state employees with 74,344 civil servants, 7,548 contract workers and 19,618 decision workers, making a total of 121,704 employees. The highest figures were attained in the year 2001, but later in 2004 and 2008, the figures rose to 124,085 and 126,482 respectively (see Table 2).

The education sectors take priority in the distribution plan :

- general education 23 837 ;
- primary and nursery 26 514 ;
- higher Education 1686 ;
- technical Education 6087 ;
- nursing 5722.

Table 3 : Growing numbers of State employees

Year	Civil servants	Contract Workers	Decision makers	TOTAL
1990	74 018	5 921	15 544	95 483
1991	71 294	5 704	14 972	91 969
1992	72 949	5 836	15 319	94 104
1993	71 269	5 702	14 966	91 937
1994	79 692	6 375	16 735	102 803
1995	80 071	6 406	16 815	103 292
1996	90 822	7 266	19 073	117 160
1997	90 762	7 261	19 060	117 083
1998	69 541	75 563	8 684	83 788
1999	79 344	6 348	16 662	102 354
2000	84 034	6 723	17 647	108 404
2001	94 344	7 548	19 812	121 704
2002	85 907	6 873	18 041	110 820
2003	88 095	7 048	18 500	113 643
2004	96 190	7 695	20 200	124 085
2005	90 064	7 205	18 913	116 183
2006	91 450	7 316	19 204	117 970
2007	92 568	7 405	19 439	119 413
2008	90 901	26 773	8 808	126 482

This resumption of the upward trend in the size of the workforce though contingent upon adjustments, resulted in the creation of an organ for the rationalization of management in certain ministries (education, public service, etc.).

The effect of the adjustment on the evolution of the workforce was short lived, as the same old causes already referred to provoked the same effect of increasing the state personnel. Could the projected decentralization accelerate the upward trend process in the size of local government workforce ?

II.3- Reasons for the development of government personnel (1910 – 1982)

The reasons for the bloated development of the cameroonian administration's staff are several and have varied with the political regimes :

i) the various colonizers were mainly looking for effective backup for their political and economic domination of the country ;

ii) post-colonial political authorities sought to bring government closer to the governed so as to ensure better supervision of citizens and to have a firm grip on the country, sometimes with greater priority being given to issues of national security[1] ;

iii) the excessive "cameroonization" of public and semi-public sectors is an important[2] factor in the development of the size of the public service ;

iv) and finally, reinforcing the workforce of the very profitable (income generating) services of the State (customs, P & T and agriculture), without forgetting the need of monitoring technical progress (P & T) or provide training to future officials (national education), have also contributed to this trend (see appendixes n°1).

---

[1] Refer to NYOGOK MPEK Germain, « La création de nouvelles circonscriptions administratives au Cameroun. Approche problématique », Mémoire Licence en Droit 1976-1977, pp. 68-73.

[2] Refer to YOUBI, « La camerounisation des cadres », *Op cit.*

CHAPTER I

GENERAL PROBLEMS OF THE PUBLIC SERVICE

- The study of general problems of management and the principles governing this domain ;
- Determining the composition of the heterogenous staff of the Administration ;
- Analysis of the civil servants' career ;
- And the list of pecuniary benefits of the civil servant supplemented by that of his rights and obligations.

I. SOURCES OF PUBLIC SERVICE LAW

Like other areas of the administrative law inspired by french law, cameroonian public service law has a duality of sources :

- First, a body of written, hierarchically heterogeneous, constitutional, statutory or regulatory rules ;

- Then, a system of fundamental jurisprudential safeguards identified by praetorian imitation of the *conseil d'Etat* and administrative courts in France by the successive administrative courts of independent Cameroon and by the litigation council of the administrative bench of the supreme court.

I.1- WRITTEN SOURCES OF PUBLIC SERVICE LAW

In Cameroon, the Constitution, the law and legislative and regulatory enactments are the main sources of the public service law.

I.1.1- The constitutional regulations of Public Service law

Those who draft and enact the Constitution in Cameroon are not averse to the prescription of rules applicable to the public service. Thus, article 25 of the 1957 statute provided that :

"within the limits of budgetary appropriations, the Prime Minister organizes the services of the State under his supervision and defines the areas of competence and the general thrust of the action of each of them."

Article 16 of the 1958 statute comes up with similar provisions :

"The Prime minister, head of cameroon government, chairs cabinet meetings, organizes the public services, makes appointments to all jobs within the State of Cameroon and ensures the proper administration of justice."

Law n° 59-2 of 18 february 1959 seeking to secure the functioning of the public service, also provided that the Prime minister appoints into all public positions within the limit of budgetary authorizations and :

"The Prime minister or ministers may by nominative order delegate their powers to officials in their respective departments, with the exception of signing or countersigning laws and decrees" (articles 28 and 29).

With independence, a more comprehensive system of public service was to develop. The president of the Republic, head of State, appears as the central pivot. In the constitution of march 4, 1960, "*he presides over the council of ministers*" (article 15), "*presides over the higher national defence councils and committees*", "*he is the head of the armed forces*", "*accredits ambassadors*" (article 16). "He makes appointments to civilian and military jobs" (article 17). The council of ministers "*must be consulted when making appointments to senior positions in the State the list of which shall be established by organic law*" (article 21). The status of judges and that of the civil service are within the "*realm of the law*" (article 23). The federal Constitution of 1961 confirmed most of these rules. The rules and regulations of the civil Service, however, ceased to belong to the realm of law (article 24).

The current Constitution, the one of 1972, which is the fundamental norm of the State, has maintained this heritage of rules on management and organization of the civil service. Following the example of the french Constitution of 4 october 1958, it sometimes enunciates the rules governing the civil service. The provisions to be considered are numerous :

- the are of new section 5 which states that the president may delegate some of his powers to members of government and some senior administration officials of the State, within the framework of their respective areas of competence ;

- that of new section 8, concerning the appointment of members of government and the determination of their areas of competence ;

- and finally, those of Article 9 which make the head of State, head of the armed forces, who accredits ambassadors and is the main holder of the power of appointments to civilian and military positions. He creates, organizes and directs all administrative services necessary to accomplish his mission, the Constitution[1] expressly provides.

In short, the Constitution of Cameroon, a fundamental norm of the State, is also the country's supreme administrative charter.

The original text revised[2] several times, maintained similar provisions that make the president the backbone of the cameroonian government, sometimes assisted by a Prime minister, head of government.

The president, through his arbitration, assures the proper functioning of public authorities (Article 5).

He may delegate some of his powers to the Prime minister, other cabinet members and some senior officials of the state administration in their respective duties. As part of an express delegation and in case of temporary incapacity, the president may instruct the Prime minister to ensure some of his functions.

The Prime minister is the head of government thus directs government action. He is responsible for the enforcement of laws. He exercises regulatory power and makes appointments to civilian jobs with the exception of those partening to the prerogatives of the president. He directs the administrative services necessary to accomplish his mission.

It should be noted *in fine* that the president of the Republic may, for a limited period and with empowerment from parliament, pass ordinances of a regulatory nature before notifying the latter.

I.1.2- Legislative rules and regulatory instruments of public service law

Other written rules make up the bulk of the legal provisions governing the civil service.

---

[1] Refer to articles 13, 20, 21 and 34 of the French Constitution of 4 october 1958.

[2] See the Constitution of the united Republic of Cameroon, National printing press, 2nd of june 1972 ;
Law nr 2008/001 of 14 april 2008 modifying and completing some dispositions of law n° 96/06 of 18 january 1996 revising the Constitution of June 2, 1972.

a. Tangible primacy of regulatory sources in Cameroon public service law

The idea of a set of predetermined rules written for the entire civil service only established itself progressively in France. The empire granted "*status*" only to certain corps of the State : foreign affairs. The july monarchy conferred status along with valuable guarantees to officers by the act of may 19, 1834. The only overall provisions applicable to all workers focused on limited issues : the act of 8 june 1953 establishing a general retirement plan and section 65 of the act of 22 april 1905 establishing the rule in the communication of records in disciplinary matters. The first general status that came into being with the Vichy regime in 1941, disappeared with the restoration of "*republican legality*" at the liberation. The october status, voted by the constituent assembly, remained in force throughout the Fourth Republic. It was replaced by the ordinance of february 4, 1959, made pursuant to a constitutional authorization under article 92 of the 1958 Constitution. The fact remains that the fundamental guarantees granted to civil servants, unlike the provisions of article 20 of the Constitution of Cameroon, fall within the realm of the law in France. According to Cameroon law, only the rules relating to the general organization of national defence remain within the competence of the lawmaker.

The jurisdiction of parliament, regarding the management of the civil service, remains very limited physically. parliament votes the budget, as well as the budgets of various government departments and that vote results in control.

Parliament controls government action through oral or written questions and the establishment of commissions of inquiry into specific cases that may well affect the activities of government departments, and consequently the administration of the State or local councils.

This fundamental difference, with regards to their material significance, establishes the primacy of regulatory sources in the corpus of norms of the cameroonian public service. This significance is confirmed by positive national law.

b. Evolution of regulatory sources of public service law

Article 51 of the statute of 1957 multiplied the status of civil servants to excess : corps of state employees serving overseas, corps of executive supplements locally organized by the high commissioner, civil servant of the cameroonian corps, civil servants and workers of the metropolitan corps, etc (section 51 of the statute of april 16, 1957).

Regulatory sources of the public service law are closely linked to the political forms of the unitary State up to today.

b.1- Plurality of statutes in the federal system

The law on autonomy characteristic of the federal system presupposes a distinction between the status of civil servants of the federal State and those of the federated states. Three regulatory statutes governed the public service during the brief period of the federation of Cameroon from 1961 to 1971. Order n° 59/70 of 27 november 1959[1] mainly inspired by the general French status of the time, governed the public service of East Cameroon. In West Cameroon, "*civil servants*" who up to then where under conditions close to those of "*private contract law*[2]," on 1st July 1969 were granted a status supplemented by legislation on pensions[3]. The latter, for convenience, incorporated the provisions in force in East Cameroon. And at the federal level, decree n° 66/DF/53 of 13 february 1966 on the general status of the federal public service, whose originality was not much different when compared to the former enactment of 1959, applied.

The de facto harmonization resulting from the similarity of the provisions of the three separate statutes formally ceased with the advent of the United Republic of Cameroon in 1972.

b.2- The unique rules and regulations of february 18, 1974

The former federal status was applied transitorily to the entire unified cameroonian public service.

Two enactments laying the beginnings of a specifically cameroonian law in several of its provisions came along in 1974 :

- decree n° 74/138 concerning the general rules and regulations of the public service and structured in a long series of 202 extremely diverse articles was signed on february 18, 1974 ;

---

[1] Refer to JOC n° 1339 du 12-12-1959, p.1701.

[2] Refer to the press conference of the minister in charge of the public service, march 11, 1966.

[3] Refer to *West Cameroon official gazette supplement,* 1969, n° 26, volume 9, 21st june 1969, Part B B 57.

- and on 26 august 1974, decree n° 74/759 standardizing the legal regime of civil servants' pensions in a consolidated text was signed.

Many other texts implementing regulations clarified this unique status with regard to personnel of the general administration, the diplomatic corps, etc.

The rules and regulations have so far remained unique. They are supplemented by other texts of a regulatory nature[1]. Decree n° 94/199 of 7 October 1994 concerning the general rules and regulations of the State public service, as amended and supplemented by decree n° 2000/287 of 12 october 2000, together with the labor code, remains the essential text applicable to contract agents of the administration.

Except where the law is silent or a legal vacuum exists, the said general rules and regulations of the public service do not apply[2] to :

- personnel recruited and managed directly by the national assembly ;
- auxiliaries of the administration, a category that is fast disappearing ;
- judges ;
- the military ;
- civil servants of the national security.

---

[1] Refer to TEKAM, *Statut général et textes d'application. Recueil des textes commentés,* Yaoundé, février 2006, 290 pages. And particularly

- law n° 92/007 of 14 april 1992 and decree n° 78/484 of 9 november 1978 ;
- decree n° 2000/684/PM of 13 september 2000 fixing the modes of attribution of the death benefit ;
- decree n° 2000/685/PM of 13 september 2000 on the organization and functioning of the permanent disciplinary board of the public Service and fixing the rules of the disciplinary procedure ;
- decree n° 2000/686/PM of 13 september 2000 on the organization and functioning of the health boards ;
- decree n° 2000/696/PM of 13 september 2000 fixing the general system of administrative competitive examinations ;
- decree n° 2000/698/PM of 13 September 2000 fixing the organization and functioning of the highest council of the public service, etc.

[2] Refer to article 10 of the general status of the Public service, above mentioned TEKAM … ;

- special status of the corps of civil servants of the penitentiary administration, decree n° 92/054 of 17 march 1992 amended by decree n° 93/846 of 22 december 1993 ;
- decree n° 2001/055 of 12 march 2001, decree n° 2001/066 of 12 march 20014 fixing the indexed scale of executives of the national security services ;
- decree n° 95/048 of march 8, 1995, amended and completed by decree n° 2004/0802 of 13 april 2004.

These corps have their special or individual status. Civil servants operating under national education are thus subject to a special status of the public service common law.

Law n° 2004/17 of 22 july 2004 orientating decentralization provides for a status for local council staff which will come about1 by way of a decree of the president of the Republic.

All these written rules do not in any way depart from the "real jurisprudential status" of the public service, inasmuch as the third source of law represented by custom is virtually absent in administrative law. At the most, there are some customs with no binding force.

I.2- SOURCES OF JURISPRUDENTIAL LAW OF THE CAMEROON PUBLIC SERVICE

The praetorian codification of rules of the Cameroon public service draws from the rich experience of French administrative courts and particularly the council of State. The highest court in Cameroon, when ruling in disputes, sometimes tries to forge national and specific solutions.

I.2.1- Resorting to existing French jurisprudential solutions

Jurisprudence was particularly developed in french administrative law for the public service ; the right of civil servants to strike partially confirmed by the lawmaker in an almost exclusive codification, up to the french law of 1963. They still inspire the right to freedom of opinion and determine the extent of the duty of loyalty and obligation to official reserve. Comprehensively, they have, with inspiration from article 65 of the law of april 22, 1905, established the rule on the communication of the dossier and generalized the principle of the rights of the defence in public service matters, not to mention recourse to the general principles of law for the benefit of civil servants and the triumph of the principle of legality.

The administrative law of Cameroon regarding the public service readily adopts these French jurisprudential solutions in several significant areas :

---

[1] Article 19 of law n° 2004/17 of july 22, 2004 on the orientation of the decentralization, JORC, july 2004, p.17.

- applying the status of civil servant (CF A6-J judgment n° 9 of october 16, 1968, Baba Youssoufa) ;

- determining jurisdiction in disciplinary procedures for civil servants (J CF AG Case n° 21 C Albert Makoube Epée versus the State of Cameroon), etc.

- irresponsibility of judicial services (CFJ judgment Awa Hadja).

It, however, does not hesitate to innovate.

I.2.2- Outline of spontaneous cameroonian jurisprudential solutions

While such solutions are still exceptional, the statutory law of the cameroonian public service may be further clarified by an outline of spontaneous, new and specific jurisprudential solutions.

The ruling of the Yaoundé administrative bench of the federal court of justice of 29 march 1972 in Mbedey Norbert C. versus the Federal Republic of Cameroon[1] is an example of an original effort of the Cameroonian judge to forge his own solutions outside the paths laid down by french case law.

The facts of this case are simple. The administration had put a government car at the disposal of Mr. Norbert Mbedey and it was stolen. The minister of finance issued a recovery order of 518 000 francs against him for the amount of damages suffered by the State. Mr. Mbedey disagreed and made an appeal to the administrative bench for this warrant to be annulled.

This tribunal deemed that it was competent to entertain the suit on the essential grounds that the recovery orders challenged by the interested party had administrative acts ; but curiously, with respect to this particular case of the worker's responsibility towards the administration, it decided to apply rules of private law and more specifically those of article 1384 of the civil code, which establishes the liability of everyone for the things entrusted in his care without the need to first establish misconduct. The Mbedey Norbert ruling is not only a landmark but also a ruling that is a demarcation from law and French case law and the creation of a genuine legal rule in the absence of a specific statute automatically determining liability. Article 21 of the finance law of june

---

[1] See *Revue Camerounaise de Droit,* n °3, p. 64. Observations Henri JACQUOT.

14, 1961, of the Republic of Cameroon cannot be invoked because the decision in question simply upholds as determining factor, the fact that "*it was Mbedey who was entrusted with custody of the vehicle and he does not prove and does not provide evidence that the vehicle at the time of theft was equipped with an ignition key and was forced*".

Case law emanating from both the council of State and the administrative bench in Cameroon has had and still has a key role in the development of a cameroonian public service law. Mr. Lekene Donfack interestingly notes its traditional areas of influence and intervention[1] :

- precedence of the general status over the special (Case n° J/Y Baba Youssoufa versus federated State, march 31, 1971) ;

- auxiliary rules for the regulation of professional competitive exams (Case n° 254/TE civil administrators' trade union versus the State of Cameroon, april 12, 1963 : any appointment into an income bracket must be made at the beginning rank of the bracket) ;

- breach of the rights of the defense ;

- communicating information from personnel file ;

- selective promotion of civil servants ;

- career record ;

- retirement and retired civil servants' scheme ;

- postings ;

- misconduct while off duty ;

- unauthorized absences from duty ;

- suspension of pay ;

- dismissal of a trainee ;

- competence of the minister of public service.Cameroonian administrative case law has built a series of innovative ideas that deserve consideration[2] and attention :

---

[1] LEKENE DONFACK Etienne Charles, *Droit administratif spécial, 1979-80*, 2e année capacité, Faculté de Droit et des Sciences Economiques, Yaoundé, pp. 23-24.

[2] DIPANDA MOUELLE Alexis, « Cour suprême du Cameroun. Répertoire chronologique de la Jurisprudence de la Cour Suprême 1ère Partie Année 1960-1980 », tome V, Droit administratif, 118pages, Imprimerie nationale.

- admissibility and inadmissibility of appeals, motions or applications made by civil servants (case n° 6 of june 23, 1964 of the State tribunal, veterans association and ruling on Bidzanga Joseph, ruling n° 3 dated 16 may 1967) ;

- the incompetency of administrative judges to entertain matters that have to do with damages caused by the administration of justice (Case n° 17 of march 16, 1967 Mfoumou Jean Baptiste) and acts occurring in a judicial proceeding (case n° 19 of march 16, 1967 january) ;

- system of competitive examinations (case n° 13 of november 8, 1973 - Yombi versus Federal Republic of Cameroon and case n° 12 of december 13, 1973 - David Tchatchouang and Tchatat versus the State of Cameroon) ;

- proceedings before the disciplinary council (ruling n° 6 of 31 may 1966 of the State tribunal, Benedict Melingui versus the state of East Cameroon - decree n° 9 of october 16, 1968, BABA Youssoufa versus the Federal State of Cameroon - ruling n° 14 of march 16, 1969, James Moukoko versus the Federated State of Eastern Cameroon. Ruling n° 3 of 28 october 1970 Jean Pierre Onana against judgment number 34/CFJ/SCAY rendered on april 30, 1968, etc.) ;

- forfeiture of civil rights and secondment for the exercise of elective office (case n° 3 of may 21, 1965, Tchoungui Zibi Elie versus Federated State of Eastern Cameroon) ;

- right of defense (case n° 13 of april 30, 1963 Nguele Jerome versus State Cameroon) ;

- fraud with the introduction of documents in the examination rooms (case n° 1 of 4 fanuary 1966 State of Cameroon versus Biba Théophile CFJ) ;

- failure to communicate the case file and right to defense (case n° 11 dated 16 march 1967 Makoma Epée Albert versus State of Cameroon) ;

- integration of a civil servant (march 18, 1967 case Mvogoh Elumat Théophile) ;

- annulment of the decision of the jury and refusal to classify a civil servant (case n° 12 of may 26, 1977, State of Cameroon versus Biakolo Max) ;

- death of a civil servant on an official assignment and condemnation of the State to pay damages to his beneficiaries (case n° 4 of february 16, 1978 State of Cameroon and attorney general of the supreme court versus Dame Elom born Danièle Perrier) ;

- sovereign power of the administration to dismiss the permanent staff or integrate a trainee (case n° 15 of april 25, 1974 EKWALL EDOUBEY Eyango Stéphane versus the Federated State of East Cameroon) ;

Revocation of the secondment of a civil servant at any time (case n° 14 of march 16, 1967 Kolle Mouang Honis versus the State of Cameroon).

This case law statute as outlined by the administrative judge may be of assistance in interpreting the basic principles of management of the public service, and may experience further developments.

II. PUBLIC SERVICE MANAGEMENT PRINCIPLES

Authority remains the fundamental principle of management of the Cameroonian public, dialectically and progressively tempered by democratic principles of recent assertion, and lastly by the spirit of good governance and "*accountability*".

II.1- THE PRINCIPLE OF AUTHORITY IN THE PUBLIC SERVICE

This first principle dominates the traditional concept of public service. It has wide ranging effects on both the organization and the operation thereof.

II.1.1- Hierarchical organization of the public service

The Cameroon public service appears primarily as a "hierarchical" order and non-egalitarian in its overall organization as in its internal structures and functioning.

Three types of hierarchy coexist here : the overall civil service entirely focused on the head of State, the corps of civil servants and the administrative structures of the government action. The general rules and regulations of the public service designate the president of the Republic, who holds the power of appointment and management of civil servants, as the supreme governing body of the public service[1]. He may delegate some of his powers to any government authority primarily to the minister in charge of the public service.

The general structure of government departments, the working place par excellence for civil servants follows the same principle of hierarchical organization. The minister, possibly assisted by a deputy minister is the head of the ministerial department. The secretary-general, in charge of monitoring department directives under the "*supreme authority of the minister*", leads a cohort of directors assisted by assistant directors who guide the work of heads of services who have at their disposal office managers responsible themselves to follow up common state employees and officials.

The public service is also organically as a hierarchical conglomerate of civil servants corps. It does not constitute an egalitarian brotherhood of peers. Civil servants are classified into categories corresponding to predetermined levels of recruitment and performance of duties. The age limit prescribed below may exceptionally and on an individual basis be rolled backwards by the Prime minister on a reasoned proposal of the minister for public service and for category A job positions.

The supreme council of the public service issues a recommendation for separate recruitments where the applicant's situation is a crucial precondition for access to the public service. Distinctions must take account of any inability to hold certain jobs.

Accordingly, it should be noted that the civil servant should be neither too young in compliance with international conventions that protect the child, nor too old to put in the regulatory period of twenty years of service prior to retirement.

An applicant for the status of civil servant must be able to present a profile of irreproachable probity presupposing a selfless style to serve and at the service of the general interest. In the past, investigations of morality and a blank "criminal record" attested to that presumption.

As for the upper age limit, it was lifted sparingly in the past. This was the case for some students who, upon graduation from the higher teacher's training college, were above age and for doctors to be

---

[1] Refer to article 14 of the 1974 general rules and regulations of the public service (decree 74/38).

integrated into the corps of the penitentiary administration[1]. That is why it must be taken into account in determining entrance into professional schools.

However, it should be noted that in the past there was mitigation of the principle of equal eligibility by former article 16 of the general rules and regulations that institutionalized the politico-realistic concept of "duties of high administrative responsibility" whose list was determined by decree and left at the discretion of government. This exemption was tempered by the fact that the status predetermined that these duties of high administrative responsibility conferred no vested right to the beneficiary and did not entail. They could not allow confirmation into a permanent income bracket of the civil Service.

It should also be noted that paragraph IV of the former article 13 of the special status of the corps of civil servants of general administration made provision for the recruitment, as senior civil administrators, and as such confirmation, "*of persons aged 40 years and above, having served for at least ten consecutive years, in posts of high political or administrative responsibility in public services, semi-public or in international organizations.*" The special status of diplomats also contained such provisions. Many persons initially benefited from such arrangements at the departure of the former president of the Republic.

Cameroonian regulations seem to have permanently moved away from such harmful aberrations. They state henceforth that any recruitment or integration into the public service "whose exclusive purpose is not intended to fill a vacancy is prohibited" and that "the appointment to any position of responsibility whatsoever does not entail integration into a civil service corps "[2].

The absoluteness of the ban through its explicit provisions suggests, beyond dispute the obsolescence, and a repeal of article 13 of decree n° 75/77 of 18 december 1975 on the special status of the corps of civil servants of the general administration which states that senior civil administrators can be chosen from outside the general administration staff among "*persons aged 40 years and above who have for at least 10 consecutive years exercised some duties in senior political or*

[1] Refer to TEKAM, *Fonction publique, Op cit.* pp. 10-11.

[2] Refer to article 85 paragraphs 1 and 2 of the general status of the Public service.

administrative positions in public or semi-public services or in international organizations."

Not only does the general take precedence over the special but also the explicit over the implicit, although this special status shows no vacuum nor silence[1] to allow the application of this benchmark status the general status of the civil service, structured in descending order of hierarchy designated by the letters A, B, C and D :

- **Category A** corresponds to management, designing or supervisory duties ;

- **Category B** corresponds to the functions of developing and implementing at a high level ;

- **Category C** jobs are specialized implementation tasks ;

- Those of category D are the common implementation tasks.

Has this hierarchy any imperative legal value ? In other words, can any official, with backing from this classification, by way of litigation challenge his assignment to duties inconsistent with his category ? Can he lay claim to any other specific function ? There are three possible answers to this question :

i) In principle, nothing in law would preclude such a claim which would only be normal, as article 10 of the general rules and regulations of 1974 provides a hierarchy of officials. The administrative judge would only have to control the match by undertaking a process of characterizing the new assignment.

ii) An explicit statutory exception should be noted : "no person is entitled to promotion by right to high administrative duties" whose list as determined by presidential order is left to the discretion of government.

iii) Even though an operation for the legal qualification of the actual job can be easily conceived, it should be noted that in terms of litigation practice, the problem has not yet arisen.

But it is increasingly likely that the problem shall be raised as the hierarchy of income brackets A, B, C and D underlies a hierarchy of job positions. Positions are attached to each category depending on whether the latter corresponds to managing, evaluative or supervisory duties ;

[1] Refer to the interpretation rules of text, article 10 paragraph 2 of the general rules and regulations.

preparatory, developmental and applicative duties ; specialized implementation or common implementation tasks of major subordination[1].

The job positions are provided for in the State budget and correspond to all those tasks, duties and responsibilities requiring special knowledge and skills.

The internal structures of the corps of civil servants follow the same logic of hierarchy and each income bracket includes grades, divided into classes organized into distinct rungs.

II.1.2- Hierarchical subordination in the public service

Civilian administrations borrow the cardinal rule of absolute obedience and subordination to hierarchy from the military administrations.

"*Every civil servant is responsible for carrying out the tasks entrusted to him. As such, he must obey individual or general instructions given by his superior in the line of duty in accordance with laws and regulations in force.*"[2]

What is the scope of the duty of obedience towards superiors of civil servants and agents who are under their orders and vis-à-vis the principle of duely abiding by the law ?

Under the laws and regulations in force, the civil servant is required, in compliance with the general rules and regulations, to obey individual or general orders given by superiors in the execution of public service tasks. Superiors in hierarchy direct the activities of workers in administrative services ; they organize in accordance with the laws in force and regulations of public services. They have power to give instructions and guidelines on civil servants under their authority. They exercise a supervisory power over the legal acts of their subordinates, expressed through the power to disallow, supervise and reform thereof. They hold an array of managerial powers over the administrative staff of the State which they appoint, recruit, assign, promote and discipline.

---

[1] Refer to articles 4 and 9 of the general rules and regulations of the public service (decree n° 94/199 of october 7, 1994 and subsequent revised texts).

[2] Refer to article 39 of the new rules and regulations, paragraph 1 and subsequent.

The obligation of obedience towards hierarchy is thus a key element of the duty of service for a civil servant.

It must be understood and emphasized that the civil servant is "*not absolved from any of his responsibilities because of the actions of those under his command, authority or control, except in cases of personal misconduct committed by them* ". The action of his subordinates does not release him from the duty of obedience towards hierarchy. He must ensure that his services and the staff under his authority fully execute orders received from above. He therefore has in this respect a real power of supervision of the execution of orders over the departments under his authority.

Can he in some cases disobey ? What are the provisions of the general rules ?[1]

"He has the duty to refuse to carry out any order that is manifestly illegal and likely to seriously compromise public interest, except on requisition by a competent authority made out with due respect to convention and legal procedure. In such a case, he is absolved of any responsibility. This also applies when he carries out legal instructions or instructions given in respect of legal procedure."

The civil servant remains subject to the principle of respect for republican legality. However, a real duty of obedience here appears. Traditionally, doctrine and statutes condition it to manifest illegality - infringement of civil liberties or influence - in the order received. Cameroon legislation conditions the existence of the duty of disobedience to the serious compromise of public interest - public disorder or disturbance in the smooth functioning of the service ; only of these two conditions put together can clear the officer of the obligation of obedience towards hierarchy. The civil servant may also be requisitioned, in which case his liability is replaced by that of the person who gave the order.

At a time when the international criminal court is in the news, that is worth remembering. The use of public law would be of extreme value in the event of litigation pending against an official of the Cameroon government.

---

[1] Refer to B. CHERIGNY (B.), « Le devoir de désobéissance à l'ordre illégal dans le contentieux disciplinaire de la Fonction publique civile », n° 4, juillet 1975.

II.2- PENETRATION OF DEMOCRATIC MANAGEMENT PRINCIPLES IN THE PUBLIC SERVICE

The principle of authority, following the evolution of political society, has had to be reconciled with the contemporary requirements of democratic management.

The particular case of France is eloquent : Article 34 of the 1958 Constitution reserving to the legislature, within a framework of political pluralism, the exclusive role to set rules on fundamental guarantees accorded to civil servants and the establishment of specialized schools, has relatively democratized access to senior administrative management. Civil servants have been given work freedom, the right to form trade unions and to strike under predetermined conditions. They have been given the right to participate in the management of (not self manage) those public services in which they work.

Progress registered in the right to parity for women is noteworthy. French law allows gender-based recruitment.

Some democratic principles are set forth by the statutory texts of the Civil Service in Cameroon.

i) Article 12 of the general rules and regulations proclaims the principle of open access to the civil service, without discrimination, to all persons of Cameroonian nationality aged at least seventeen (17) and thirty-five (35) at most for civil servants of categories A and B, and at least seventeen years and not more than thirty years for civil servants of categories C and D. Applicants must meet the physical requirements for the job applied for, must not have been sentenced for any crime or probity offence including theft, forgery, influence peddling, swindling, fraud, corruption, misappropriation of public funds or abuse of trust ; of a sentence accompanied with one of the payment deadlines.

ii) Article 27 of the revised General Rules and Regulations grants the civil servant the enjoyment of rights and freedoms granted to every other citizen. He enjoys these rights and freedoms within the framework of the laws in force. He may join a political or cultural association, or a legally recognized trade union to represent and defend his career interests. He is thus under obligation to respect the authority of the State and public order.

However, it should be noted that the revised rules innovate by requiring of the holders of certain functions, loyalty to the institutions of the Republic or absolute public neutrality. Such functions shall be the subject of a special text.

What are those functions that require only loyalty and those where simple political neutrality would suffice ? The answer to this question would lead to the depolarization of the Cameroon public service.

iii) The general rules and regulations of the public service (new Article 34) grants employees a right to participate in the management of their career and in the running of public services :

"Civil servants shall participate in the drawing up of the rules and regulations governing their career or the running of government services through their elected representatives in consultative boards.

They shall take part, where applicable, in the definition and management of social, cultural, sports and leisure programmes that are intended for them or which they themselves organize."

To this effect, some consultative bodies in charge of the running of the Public Service observe parity with equal representation from the administration and from the civil servants. These organs include : joint administrative commissions, standing disciplinary council, higher council of the public service and health[1] boards.

A special text of the Prime minister head of government establishes the modalities of this participation[2] :

- civil servants are involved in the drawing up of statutory rules related to their career or the running of public services when it concerns any draft text on the situation of civil servants, issues concerning the rights and obligations of civil servants, policy guidelines for continuing professional development, plans to reorganize the civil service leading to workforce expansion or jobs cuts, any policy revising civil servants salaries and benefits, any proposed amendment to the status of the civil service of the State and to particular or special status, the promotion of civil servants, rewards, and the discipline of civil servants ; the elected representatives of civil servants sit in the management organs of the

---

[1] Successively refer to articles 34, 86, 87, 88, 89 and 90 of the revised general rules and regulations.

[2] Refer to decree n° 2000/694/PM of september 13, 2000 ruling the right to participation, refer to TEKAM *Op cit.* pp. 187-191.

public service (higher council of the public service, administrative boards, the permanent disciplinary council) ;

- they may form legally recognized trade unions thereby sanctioning in this status an old position of the French council of State ;

- civil servants define and manage social, cultural, sporting and leisure initiatives through the associations they create within their area of activity or within the structures meant for the promotion of activities created by the administration. The resources of these associations come from the members.

The above provisions apply to State employees under the labour code, pending subject to the concurrent application of provisions specific to this category of personnel.

In the past, the mode of election of such elected representatives of civil servants in these joint bodies - single round single candidate ballot - was perfectly democratic although conditioned by appointments made by the minister of public service in a separate order.

iv) The ban prohibiting any mention in his professional record or document of his opinions or political beliefs, trade union, philosophical or religious affiliation or belonging or non belonging to a trade union or political party, is part of this statutory policy of empowering and democratizing the civil service. Any constitution of an "Edwige" type file is as such prohibited[1].

v) Administrative competitive exams are all modes of recruitment of civil servants who are selected in order to fill available job gaps in the civil service. This recruitment method extends to direct competitive exams, professional competitive exams, special competitive exams and competitive exams for scholarships for training or further training courses.

The legal status of the civil servant seems circumscribed by contradictory imperatives - those that are traditional by dint of the principle of authority necessary for efficiency and those that are contemporary as required by democratization in any political society. A number of state agencies are responsible for implementing these principles, which are now complemented by other new principles.

---

[1] Refer to the highly contested file case « Edwige » in France.

II.3- THE PRINCIPLES OF GOOD GOVERNANCE AND "ACCOUNTABILITY"

Globalization has had a major effect on the management of State personnel, civil servants and agents. It has fostered the emergence of the principles inherent in good governance and the principle of regular accountability[1].

The establishment of a national governance programme was announced in a message to the nation on december 31, 1985, by the president of the Republic.

What is the institutional framework of this programme and its evolution ? What is its impact on the management of the state's administration, in particular the career of civil servants and of State contract workers ?

A Prime ministerial decree established a National governance programme in cameroon (PNG) [2] which was soon transformed into a national programme for governance and the fight against corruption (PNGL) [3]. Its work focuses primarily on the following sectors : public administration, decentralization, justice, economic, financial and social management and the participation of citizens and the civil society in the

---

[1] See successively :
- services du Premier ministre – *Mémorandum sur la bonne gouvernance et les Droits de l'Homme au Cameroun*, novembre 2000, bilingue, République du Cameroun, 45 pages.
- République du Cameroun (services du Premier ministre), *Programme national de bonne gouvernance*, Yaoundé, 2004, 143 pages.
- Order n° 032/PM of august 11, 1998 organizing the institutional frame of execution of the first part of the National Programme of Governance.
- Order n° 19/PM of february 13, 2003 creating follow-up committees on the implementation of the National de Programme of Governance.
- Decision n° 001/CAB/PM of may 27, 2003 on the constitution of the steering committee of the National Programme of Governance.
- Decision n° 005/CAB/PM of august 11, 2005 on the constitution of the PNGL pilot committee.

[2] Successively refer to :
- order n° 32/PM of august 11, 1998 and
- decision n° 05/CAB/PM of august 11, 2005.

[3] Successively refer to :
- order n° 032/PM of august 11, 1998 and
- decision n° 005/CAB/PM of august 11, 2005.

management of public affairs. The programme is designed and implemented.

The work of the first phase is being controlled, directed and coordinated by a steering committee, five sectoral committees and headed by a national coordinator.

The steering committee chaired by the Prime minister and head of government has as ex-officio members the ministers of economy, finance, justice, administrative reform, territoriala and the president of the sectoral committee on civil society, senior State officials and representatives of civil society nominated *intuitu personna* are the other members of the steering committee.

The national coordinator is assisted by a deputy coordinator. The chairman of the steering committee may invite or co-opt national or international technical cooperation experts to participate in the proceedings of the steering committee.

Ministers who are members preside ex officio the sectoral committees regarding the administration, decentralization, justice, the economy and finance, with regards to their respective duties.

Sectoral committees include a technical coordinator and members co-opted by the Prime minister and ministers of attachment. The technical coordinators are responsible for the technical conduct of the work scheduled in their sectoral committees. They work in conjunction with the national coordinator.

Furthermore, there is a monitoring committee for the national programme on good governance in every ministry. It is responsible for monitoring the implementation of the actions listed on the National Governance Programme at the level of the ministry and is placed under the authority of the Minister and chaired by the Secretary General of that ministry. The monitoring unit of the Department handles its secretariat.

The composition of the steering committee was greatly improved in 2003 with the expansion of its membership to other ministries (education, economic affairs, employment, labour and social welfare, women empowerment, communication, youth, sports and physical education). Important social groups were also invited to attend : civil society, syndustricam, chamber of commerce, industry and handicrafts, national commission on human rights and fundamental freedoms, the league for woman and child education, and religious denominations[1].

The impact of PNGL on the functioning of the cameroonian administration is now showing to be important.

The national governance programme has identified five priority areas :

- the establishment of a government that truly serves the public ;
- consolidation of the rule of law through the establishment of an enabling legal and judicial environment that guarantees the safety of persons, goods and investments ;
- promoting a culture of responsibility in economic, financial and social management and the obligation to accountability ; in the management of state affaires ;
- enhancing transparency in governance by fighting against corruption ;
- the establishment of decentralized structures for effective and efficient participation of people in their governance (decentralization).

Several actions have been completed or were underway to enhance the efficiency of the authority :

- creation of an institutional and legal framework for the management of State personnel with the decentralization of personnel management in some departments, the development of an integrated information management system for state personnel and pay (SIGIPES), the organization of administration / public relations and services ;
- consolidation of the rule of law with the reinforcement of the guarantee, without discrimination, of civil and political rights, the assurance of equal access to justice and security of investments (effective implementation of the OHADA law) the set up of a new judiciary in accordance with new constitutional provisions, the strengthening of the State/private sector partnership. Several of such projects or actions, have thus been geared towards, among other things, improving the procurement system with the aim of controlling the award of public contracts and expenditure, and reducing corruption. A regulatory agency

---

[1] Order n° 001/CAB/PM of may 27, 2003 on the constitution of the steering committee of the National Programme of governance.
Order n° 005/CAB/PM of august 11, 2005 on the constitution of the steering committee of the National Programme of governance and fight against corruption.

was set up, the responsibility of contracting authorities increased and legislation reviewed.

- the fight against corruption was accelerated by setting up a system of transparency and accountability, the adoption of mechanisms to identify, prevent and combat corruption : the National anti-corruption committee (CONAC), National agency for financial investigation (ANIF) and new criminal provisions.

Many significant actions have been achieved under the auspices of good governance and the principle of accountability. They are :

- the systematic introduction of thorough investigations into the behaviour and morals of future State personnel preferably between short-listing and the final result of competitive examinations ;

- the establishment and enforcement of the career plan of the corps thereby moralizing appointments and promotions ;

- the application of the system of rotation of responsibilities within the same government services ;

- setting a mandate for the exercise of certain duties, including the obligation to results spelled out beforehand in the specifications ;

- harmonization of the rules and regulations of the various corps for the purpose of putting them on a level play ground with regard to professional advancement and retirement or other benefits ;

- upgrading the purchasing power of public officials ;

- Effective enforcement of legislation relating to allowances and awards and their effective implementation ;

- modalities for the control and monitoring of services and staff with a follow-up of their lifestyle and the declaration by senior officials of their assets ;

- strict application of sanctions in the fight against corruption[1] ;

- the creation within government departments of units for the fight against corruption with entitlement to disclosure of all documents and information necessary for the accomplishment of their missions ;

- institutionalization in the general rules and regulations of the civil service of the disciplinary procedure with a better definition of professional misconduct, a scale of penalties (*milla peina sin lege*).

---

[1] Refer to the criminal sanctions, articles 134, 134 bis, 312, 315, 136 and 137 of the cameroonian penal code, etc.

The decentralization component also occupies an important place in the action plan of the national programme on governance and the fight against corruption.

A guiding law for decentralization, as well as laws relating to the regions, and to the rules applying to local councils was voted. A draft decree establishing the status of municipal staff and municipal administrators (CEFAM) was elaborated.

Attempts at sharing decision-making power with the people have been launched, and the people informed on public affairs. Manuals of administrative procedures have been developed to help the public (ministry of land tenure, for example).

The new evaluation system for State employees is under study and the electronic interface, called "AQUARIUM", coupled with SIGIPES allows users to monitor real-time the progress of their files, thus symbolizing the penetration of the spirit of good governance in managing the civil service.

III. MANAGING STRUCTURES OF THE PUBLIC SERVICE

The managing structures of the Cameroon public service, inspired by those of the French Republic are largely beholden to the nature of the presidential political system in Cameroon. They are grouped into presidential, governmental and consultative management organs.

III.1- PRESIDENTIAL ORGANS OF THE PUBLIC SERVICE MANAGEMENT

The 1972 Constitution, amended several times, makes the president the real cornerstone of the edifice of the cameroonian administration[1].

In this regard, related constitutional rules should be recalled[2] :

- he ensures through his arbitration the regular functioning of Government ;

[1] Refer to Laws n° 2008/001 of april 14, 2008, n° 96/06 of january 18, 1996 on the revision of the Constitution of 2nd june 1972, n° 79-2 of 29th june 1979, law 75/1 of may 9, 1975.

[2] Articles 5, 6, 8, 9, 10 of the revised 1972 Constitution.

- he is the guarantor of national independence, territorial integrity, permanence and continuity of the state, respect for treaties and international agreements ;

- he is the Head of the armed forces ;

- he ensures the internal and external security of the Republic ;

- he accredits ambassadors and extraordinary envoys to foreign powers and ambassadors and envoys are accredited to him ;

- he exercises regulatory power ;

- he creates and organizes public services of the State ;

- he makes appointments to civil and military jobs of the State ;

- he confers decorations and honorary distinctions.

Moreover, he can declare a state of emergency that allows him to exercise special powers provided by the law and the state of emergency that enables him to take all necessary measures. The state of emergency and the state of exception may in one or several ways influence the functioning of public services and State administration[1].

The general rules and regulations of the public service or the particular or special rules and regulations make him the supreme administrative authority.

Article 2 of the general rules and regulations of the public service stipulates that the civil service is "*under the authority of the president of the Republic*."

It is also provided that orders of the president of the Republic determine the particular or special rules and regulations of the various corps of civil servants regulated by the general rules and regulations. The former as has been stated, may repeal the latter, especially as regards the right to strike.

The president confers honorary titles upon proposals from the Prime minister, accompanied by a detailed report and the opinion of the joint administrative board for the individual decisions involving advancements, the granting of awards and dismissals.

He fixes the conditions for entitlement to pension paid by the treasury or any other retirement fund.

---

[1] See in reference the French jurisprudence of the Conseil d'Etat Rubin de Servins.

He may waive the rules for determining the age limit for admission to retirement based on the nature or specificity of certain duties (article 124, paragraph 2).

He may by decision increase fivefold the death benefit in case of death following an accident attributable to duty or occurring by reason of or during duty, to the assigns of magistrates, military personnel and national security staff.

The presidency, as per the rules and regulations, authorizes any movement for an official mission abroad. The agreement to fully or partially support the costs of this displacement does not exempt the employee from the substantive requirement of obtaining the express exit permission. For reasons of expediency, this procedure has been relaxed and of the Prime minister authorised to handle certain categories of workers.

The president has his own attributions that allow him to ensure the management policy that he defines.

He disposes of a wide range of services and authorities, from the presidency to the government and heads of peripheral administrative districts.

III.1.1 The presidency of the Republic

The presidency of the Republic comprises several bodies capable of ensuring the implementation of the policy promoted by the head of State in the management of State personnel.

a. The General Secretariat

The initial founding texts provided that the general secretariat shall "*investigate all matters submitted to the sanction of the Head of State and the records entrusted to them by the president of the Republic*". "*It monitors the implementation of decisions taken by the head of State*"[1].

---

[1] Refer to decree n° 84-29 of february 4, 1984 organizing the government and decree n° 84/30 of february 4, organizing the presidency of the Republic, JORC n° 3, 14 february 1984, pp. 429-443.

M. Kamdem[1] qualifies the secretary general as a president in dashes. For me, he is certainly "*the senior technical assistant of the head of State, in matters including management of the administration.*"

This initial general approach has constantly been maintained despite the creation of the post of the Prime minister. Mr. Binyoum, referring to the general secretariat, spoke of a "super government." [2] Mr. Jean Claude Kamdem emphasizes its coordination, legal advisory functions and privileged collaboration with the president of the Republic.

The general secretariat is placed under the authority of a secretary general with the rank of minister of State and is assisted by three assistant secretaries-general with the rank and privileges of a minister and sometimes vice-minister. It seems to be the equivalent of presidential affairs departments which is common in english speaking countries. And the institution continues to grow.

Internal services of the general secretariat include the travel service, the regulatory legislative filing registry, the printing press of the palace, the computer unit, the department of human resources, the secretariat of the ministerial councils, the presidential mail directorate, the language and bilingualism department, the directorate of the official gazette and the directorate of general affairs[3].

The secretary general is appointed by the president of the Republic. His duty, among others things, is to receive all guidelines for the definition of national policy from the president of the Republic, and implement the decisions taken by the president of the Republic. He coordinates those government departments attached to the presidency. He studies all files assigned to him by the president of the Republic and monitors the execution of instructions. He submits, for the signature of the president, draft acts of any kind emanating either from the Prime minister's office or government departments attached to the presidency. In conjunction with the secretary general of the Prime minister's office, he provides the formatting for draft laws for submission to parliament. He is also responsible for liaison with other republican institutions

---

[1] KAMDEM (J.C), *Institutions administratives et Droit Administratif*, Tome I pp. 91-93.

[2] BINYOUM (J.), *Droit administratif*, Faculté de Droit et des Sciences économiques (2è Année Licence), p.40.

[3] Refer to decree n° 098/273 of 22 october 1998 re-organizing the presidency of the Republic.

particularly with the constitutional council, the supreme court, the economic and social council and the supreme State control.

The internal divisions' functioning are determined by special memorandum (memo n° 002/CAB/PR of 28 april 2003).

The head of State, with the general secretariat, disposes of a veritable conglomerate of skills : technical advisers, official representatives and administrative assistants committed to carry out his public service management policy. He may request specific tasks of these services for the development and implementation of this policy.

A number of particularly sensitive governments departments are attached to the general secretariat :

- general delegation for national security as regards its administration ;

- National research centre (CENER) ;

- presidential security responsible for the head of State's bodyguard ;

- the secretariat of the supreme judicial council which is a special corps of civil servants.

b. The Civil Cabinet

The civil cabinet is responsible for private matters, protocol, official visits and audiences of the president of the Republic.

c. The minister delegate in charge of (the services of) State Control

He is responsible for supreme control, management of public finance in public services, government institutions and para-statal structures administrative and financial plans.

In the past, he audited public accounts and contributed to the punishment of accounting officers, payment authorizers and appropriations managers as provided by the laws and regulations. The appearance of the audit bench (of the Supreme court) has somewhat changed these functions by transferring enforcement of accountability to this bench of the Supreme court.

d. Ministers in charge of missions and special advisers

They all perform every assignment or task entrusted to them by the president of the Republic. On the face of it nothing rules out issues relating to the public service.

The presidency, the highest structure of government, remains a linchpin in the organization of the civil service, starting from the functions of head of State in this area.

III.1.2- Government organs

The office of the Prime minister, the minister of public service and administrative reform and the heads of ministerial departments all constitute governmental services where the public service is managed.

a. The Office of the Prime minister

The cameroonian Constitution of 1972, amended, several times authorizes the head of State to delegate certain powers to the Prime minister, other government members and some senior state officials and this within their respective duties (article 10, paragraphs 2 and 3). He may, in the case of temporary incapacity, ask the Prime minister to ensure some of his functions by express delegation.

The Prime minister is the head of government. He directs government action and he is responsible for the enforcement of laws. He exercises regulatory power and makes appointments to civilian jobs with the exception of those partnering to the prerogatives of the President of the Republic in this field. He directs all administrative services necessary for the accomplishment his mission. He may in turn delegate his powers to other members of government and senior staff officials.

Internal services of the Prime minister are made up of a general secretariat, a secretariat for cabinet meetings, a law and regulations directorate, an administrative and claims department, a government mail and archives department and general affairs department. Some of these structures may be involved in the process of managing the public service.

The general secretariat thus monitors the implementation of decisions taken by the Prime minister. It investigates and examines files assigned by the latter. It ensures monitoring of the implementation of laws and regulations. It is the judicial council of the government.

The department of administrative affairs and claims is responsible for the supervision of the enforcement of regulations and instruments that need to be signed, the supervision of the enforcement of rules and regulations governing State personnel, administrative disputes brought before the Prime minister and the study of petitions made to him.

The department of government mail and archives keeps files and archives.

The office of the Prime minister also included related services :

- The highest authority of the public service which was never implemented ;

- the national commission on human rights and fundamental freedoms ;

- the national communication council.

The system put in place has gradually been run in for the benefit of the Prime minister. A decree of application of constitutional provisions has equipped the Prime minister with the power to control all public services, except those attached to the presidency of the Republic, like national defence, relations with the assemblies, State control services, State security and national security. He used to exercise regulatory authority by order, by circulars, individual acts in the form of decrees or orders of the Prime minister. Integration and dismissal of civil servants in category A, and the appointment of heads of services, deputy directors and now directors, fell within his remit. The range of actions has increased with elevation in hierarchy.

b. The Minister in charge of the public service

Since the introduction of the unitary state, a single government department is responsible for the civil service.

Current regulations re-enacted almost verbatim already old[1] provisions :

- management of civil servants and State employees, except for officers of the national security and armed forces, judiciary and penitentiary administration personnel subject to the powers delegated to other ministerial departments ;

---

[1] Refer to NLEP, *L'administration Publique camerounaise, Op. cit.*

- the preparation of legislation or regulations on the status of State employees ;

- coordination of training activities for State employees and civil servants ;

- the diligence of disciplinary actions against civil servants and public agents under the conditions specified in the regulations ;

- all studies related to the changing needs and resources in State workers ;

- civil service claims.

It is the state council on matters of administrative reform organization.

As such, he studies and makes proposals to government aimed at improving the cost-efficiency ratio in the public services and at expediting the processing of administrative records.

He also oversees the national school of administration and magistracy and the higher institute of public management.

He has a general secretariat and a highly structured ministerial department. In 1971, it comprised a central organization and method section responsible for conducting studies on organizational problems and improving the functioning of services.

c. Other Heads of ministerial departments

Roger Gabriel Nlep brilliantly describes the structure of the ministerial department in administrative systems in Africa resulting from the dual phenomenon of authority and hierarchy.

The head of a ministerial department has a secretariat and a department of human resources responsible for the management of personnel under his authority.

The personnel management powers of the minister are expanding gradually. A more flexible, diligent and transparent institutional and legal framework for personnel management has been gradually implemented.

Improving service management and relationships between government and users, promoting respect for ethics and professional ethics and the development of an information system for integrated management of State personnel and payroll (SIGIPES) have made notable leaps towards the decentralizing of the management of administrative staff in certain departments (Ministry of finance and budget, Ministry of public service and administrative reform, of secondary education and Ministry of public health).

These reforms now allow these departments to manage civil servants and State employees at their disposal. Data management is made more reliable and transparent. Integrations (tenure), advancements and retirements are addressed directly at this level.

III.1.3- The heads of peripheral administrative districts

a. Regional governors

The existence of decentralized administrative organizations allows in the ten regions of the Republic of Cameroon regional governors to play a vital management role in matters of public administration.

a.1- The governor, government representative

In this capacity, he represents the government and individual ministers, particularly the minister of public service. He represents the State in court, more especially in disputes. He generally performs the tasks assigned by the President and which may be of interest to the public service or public servants in the region : the head of State being the supreme head of the administration. He may by way of regional orders take individual decisions.

a.2- The Governor, coordinator of regional civil services

The governor, under the authority of competent ministers, ensures the general supervision and coordination of the activity of regional services of the State except those of the judiciary which are within the competence of the keeper of the seals.

supervisory power in many respects entails managerial prerogatives for the public service :

- right of sending copies of letters addressed by members of government to their respective regional representatives and which may well be disciplinary correspondences concerning promotion or proposing the transfer of regional officials ;

- right to carry out all inspections, investigations and coordination measures necessary for the accomplishment of his mission ;

- chairs by right, all technical administrative meetings or committees.

The sectoral adjustment plan introduced a degree of devolution mainly regarding the education sector.

a.3- The governor as government's informant

Heads of regional departments must keep the governor informed of all matters within their jurisdiction and of particular importance for the region. He has the right to request such information. The scope of such a prerogative should be assessed in conjunction with his power to evaluate all civil servants stationed in the region.

a.4- The governor as holder of the requisition right

The governor may, in case of an infringement to the internal or external security of the State or to public order, require any officer or competent authority to take all necessary actions towards establishing the crimes and bringing the offenders to court.

In short, the governor is the "president in the region" for the civilian government workers under his authority. He has a legal and administrative division in charge of, among other tasks, centralizing mark-sheets of civil servants in the region, even for those supervised by other administrative authorities.

b. Other heads of administrative units

The regional governor is assisted in his task by Senior divisional officers (SDOs) and Divisional officers (DOs) who work under his authority. Municipal officials at their own level perform some managerial functions.

b.1- The Senior divisional officer (SDO)

The SDO in the division is the representative of both the government and of each minister. He represents the minister for public service. He provides overall supervision for civilian services within his department, except for those falling under the keeper of Seals for the exercise of justice. He appreciates the mark-sheets of all officials of departments under his control. He has a right to investigate and to be sent copies of letters addressed to members of government or by the latter to regional services. He coordinates his services by taking measures he deems necessary. He may give written instructions but it is up to him to report to the competent ministers. However, decisions about services are taken by him only on proposals by the local officials responsible for the effective preparation of those decisions. By right, he presides over all or divisional administrative or technical meetings or commissions.

The governor may delegate his powers to the SDO. Like the governor, he is entitled, within the division to requisition any officer or competent authority to take all action necessary towards establishing the crimes and offenses against the internal or external security of the State and bringing the perpetrators to the courts in the manner and time specified by the legislation in force.

He has the police, gendarmerie and army at his disposal under conditions laid down by the regulations in force. He makes prefectorial orders.

Within the division he oversees and coordinates civilian Government services of the State.

b.2- The Divisional officer (DO)

As the representative of government in his constituency, he is in charge of the maintenance of order, enforcement of laws, regulations and government decisions and the supervision and coordination of the activities of public services based in his constituency.

Cameroonian administrative case law has clarified that the authority exercised by DOs, SDOs and Heads of districts, as it is not attached to their rank, is delegated to them in the name of the executive (CFJ/AP/ decision n° 5 of march 31, 1971 in the matter of Federated State of East Cameroon versus Youssoufa Baba).

b.3- Municipal executives

Government delegates in some municipalities, mayors and their deputies, at their respective levels, are called to exercise certain management powers over public officials.

The mayor is responsible for appointments to municipal jobs and for implementing the decisions of the city council.

The mayor recruits, suspends and dismisses those staff governed under labour law and collective agreements. He enforces the standard schedule municipal jobs taking into account the size of the various municipalities. He is assisted by a secretary general, main coordinator of the municipal administrative services.

The Government delegate at the level of the urban council exercises those functions exercised by the mayor in a town.

A special text of the minister for local authorities determined the procedures for the delegation of powers by mayors and government delegates to their respective assistants in various sectors of activity : health, education, sports and youth, etc...

III.1.4- Heads of autonomous institutions

The cameroonian government has several administrations with broad managerial autonomy : university institutions, national security. These two examples deserve special consideration.

a. The delegate general for national security

A special text organizes the general delegation for national security[1]. National security is a "*command and administration corps*" under the authority of the president of the Republic who is the supreme commander and whose action covers the entire national territory.

National security's fundamental mission is to ensure respect and protection of institutions, civil liberties, persons and property. It ensures compliance with laws and regulations. It contributes to the administrative and judicial enforcement of law and order. It also contributes, as a regular force, to national defence.

To this end, it is responsible for internal and external security of the State ; research, the establishment of violations of criminal laws and bringing offenders before the criminal courts. It is also in charge of maintaining order and public peace, protection, security and public safety especially in urban areas. It participates in the fight against domestic, international and transnational crime, intelligence and security information missions, protection and intervention involving contacts with people in the context of national defence.

It has already been stressed that national security falls under the direct authority of the president of the Republic. However, it performs the tasks assigned by government authorities within their respective jurisdictions, in conformity with the directives of the president of the Republic. It acts on the initiative of its commanding officer or its various officials in strict compliance with their duties.

---

[1] Refer to decree n° 83-378 of august 19, 1983.

On defence and in an operational situation, the national security receives orders from the president of the Republic and works closely with the ministries in charge of defence and territorial administration. Its units can be put at the disposal of specially constituted operational commands.

The delegate general for national security is answerable to the president of the Republic, for whom he performs a permanent mission of information. He obtains from him all the delegations of signature necessary to accomplish his missions.

His administrative role in managing the body of the national security is most important :

- he ensures the training and equipping of personnel ;

- he directs and supervises the activities of services ;

- he draws up programmes for the equipment and infrastructure facilities of national security ;

- he is responsible for the preparation and execution of the budget of national security.

The administration of the general delegation for national security comprises many complex structures.

Specialized structures contribute to its missions as a command corps :

- a **general inspectorate responsible** for all evaluation, inspection or supervision **missions** entrusted by the head of the corps and which polices the police through the special division for the supervision of services ;

- a **directorate of territorial surveillance for missions of protection thereof** ;

- a **central command for mobile intervention units** responsible for maintaining law and order throughout the national territory, which is a permanent pool of intervention ;

- the **special operation unit in charge of police raids**, commando and anti-commando against dangerous individuals or organized gangs of criminals, the neutralization of frantic armed persons. It is equally in charge of actions against all forms of mutiny, the safety of some convoys, interventions against air piracy and all terrorist actions, the removal, neutralization or destruction of objects and booby-trapped or suspicious objects and bombs, the specific training of interventions service personnel, etc ;

- an **Interpol national central bureau** (BCNI) which is a structure for international police cooperation[1] ;

- a **Communications and public relations unit** and a division for official trips and ceremonies.

The central administration also includes several management structures : **a *general secretariat***, a directorate of human resources, a directorate of finance, information management and logistics, a directorate of public security, a **directorate of general intelligence**, a directorate of judicial police, a directorate of health, a directorate of training, a national police academy, police training and practicing centres, a division of sports and social works, a division of transmissions and a permanent secretariat of the disciplinary council.

The delegate general for national security, under the supervision of the president and to some extent by the relay of the general secretariat of the presidency is a real head of an autonomous organization. He has the powers and is assisted by a secretary general and a finance controller on secondment from the ministry of finance.

b. University rectors

Despite the supervision by the minister of higher education which ensures the development and implementation of the government policy for organization, operation and control in this area, the chancellor of academic orders and rectors of Universities appear to be the successors of the chancellor of the University, formerly the head of an original administrative organization. The tradition of autonomy of academic institutions placed him at the head of the University of Yaoundé.

He was the government delegate to the University. Managerial powers in respect of teaching and administrative staff at his disposal were immense. He chaired the board of directors and the permanent section of the board of directors. He ensured the general management of the University and heads of colleges were answerable to him. He received all correspondences addressed to the University. He led the general and financial administration of the University. He chaired the boards of

---

[1] See details in 21 to 25 of decree n° 2001/003 organizing the General delegation of national security.

directors, development and orientation meetings of colleges and institutes of the University. He appointed heads of departments after establishing the need and consulting the vice-chancellor. He had disciplinary action within the University of Yaoundé and a general entitlement to give verbal or written warnings.

A rector is placed at the head of each University.

He is appointed by presidential decree, chosen among the faculty members of university institutions with the rank of senior lecturer. It should be noted that he has retained significant prerogatives :

- he runs the University on administrative and academic matters ; he ensures the implementation of the resolutions of the University board of governors ; he is responsible of its external relations, he executes the budget of the University ; presides over the board of directors, development as well as orientation meetings ; he receives the minutes of boards and meetings of the various institutions ; he recruits the administrative staff and support staff, ensures the recruitment of lecturers for the whole University, metes out disciplinary sanctions according to the rules and regulations in force ; puts University personnel on mission within the country and abroad ; sees to the running of the colleges of the University ; he may at this level take measures to re-establish order and without delay refer the matter to the minister of higher education ; he disposes of the general right to query the staff of the University in private and in public according to the regulations in force ; he can delegate his signature in specific domains and according to particular modalities to the secretary general of the University and to the heads of establishments when the need arises ;

- in the economic perspectives, he ensures conferment of grades and titles and with the supervisory minister signs the certificates awarded by the University, he sees to the implementation of teaching and research programmes of the University ; he approves the organisation and functioning of teaching units and research teams associated at the level of inter university cooperation ; he represents the University at court in all circumstances ; organises and runs University cooperation.

Four working commissions are created by the rector :

- a commission for university planning and development ;

- a commission for cultural, sporting and associative activities ;

- a council for publications, documentation and the library ;

- a coordination meeting of the administrative services of the rectorale as well as for the affiliated establishments.

The administrations assisting them are powerful, many and complex : the general secretariat ; the department of academic affairs and cooperation ; the department of infrastructure, planning and development ; the University centre for housing, catering and bursaries ; the department of administrative and financial affairs ; the socio-medical[1] centre, the book-keeping agency.

The minister of higher education is the chancellor of academic orders. His powers are vast[2] :

- he harmonises university courses ;

- he ensures supervision of courses dispensed by university institutions ;

- with the heads of university institutions he signs certificates ;

- he sees to it that freedom and liberty are guaranteed ;

- he fixes the teaching programmes, the study and examination system ;

- on the proposal of the head of university institution concerned, he metes out disciplinary sanctions as laid down by the texts ;

- he chairs the conference of heads of establishments ;

- and he may make reports in extraordinary session of the board of governors of the university institutions.

In spite of the designation of external personalities as chairpersons of the board of governors in universities, rectors still remain the powerful « chiefs » of a strongly autonomous administration even with the presence of the chancellor of academic orders.

---

[1] Refer to decree n° 93/036 of january 29, 1993 organizing the administrative and academic of the University of Yaoundé I – Chapter III : articles 57 to 106.

[2] Refer to decree n° 93/036 of january 29, 1993 organizing the administrative and academic of the University of Yaoundé II.

III.2- CONSULTATIVE MANAGEMENT ORGANS OF THE PUBLIC SERVICE

The general rules and regulations of the public service (article 17) institute three kinds of consultative organs : the higher council of the public service, the joint administrative boards, the health boards and the permanent public service disciplinary board.

Through these organs, the civil servant exercises his right to participate in the management of the public service.

III.2.1- The higher council of the public service

The higher council of the public service appears as a joint consultative organ assisting government authorities.

a. A joint consultative organ

This joint organ comprises twenty four members : twelve (12) members representing the administration and twelve (12) representing public service workers who are chosen among the staff representatives of the joint administrative committees at the ratio of three representatives for each of the categories, according to the following distribution :

- one (1) representative category A-2nd grade ;
- two (2) representatives category A-1st^{r} grade ;
- one (1) representative category B-2nd grade ;
- two (2) representatives category B-1st^{r} grade.

The representatives of civil servants to the higher council of the public service are elected on a single candidate majority ballot in a single round for a three year mandate. The prorogation of the mandate of joint administrative committees automatically implies that of the staff representatives sitting in the higher council. The elections are organized by the minister in charge of the public service. This election is certified by a decision of the Prime minister. It follows the rules laid down for the election of representatives.

The representatives of the administration are made up of the ministers in charge of the public service, territorial administration, national education (basic education and secondary education), justice, social affairs, work, supreme state control, women affairs and three (3) personalities chosen by the Prime minister because of their expertise.

The higher council of the public service is presided over by the Prime minister head of government.

Its remits are basically consultative and for suggestions :

- It hears all matters relating to the public service ;

- It also examines all draft bills on the condition of civil servants, all questions relating to the rights and obligations of civil servants ; on the orientations of the continuous professional training policy in the public service ; any plan to reorganize the public service leading to an increase or reduction in the size of staff ; any policy revising civil servants' wages as well as the social benefits they are entitled to ; and any plan to amend the general rules and regulations of the public service.

The higher council of the public service rules on appeals entered against disciplinary sanctions, temporary suspension from service for durations of more than four (4) months, a demotion in category or rank and dismissal for professional shortcomings.

Within the framework of its remit, the higher council expresses opinions or makes recommendations.

Without coming out in favour of the necessarily corresponding compliant character of these opinions and recommendations, the latter remains the working range for a real inter-ministerial committee complemented by the consultation of civil servants.

The higher council of the public service can be convened by the Prime minister or by at least one third of its members on general matters. It can convene when a matter is brought before it by a civil servant accused in a disciplinary procedure.

The higher council of the public service is organized and operates under special conditions.

It sits in plenary sessions, authorized only to express opinions and make recommendations on matters referred to the council. In that case, it is convened by its president at least twice (2) a year. Members are notified of such meetings at least fifteen (15) days before the meeting date. It can only hold validly when at least two thirds (2/3) of its members are present. The opinions and the recommendations are adopted on a simple majority of the members present, the chairman having a casting vote.

Minutes are drawn at the end of every meeting and signed by all the members. Its secretariat is handled by the directorate in charge of legal matters at the ministry of the public service.

A commission of inquiry and a committee for appeals operate within the higher council. The commission of inquiry is charged with preparing files for deliberations in plenary meeting.

The appeals committee prepares files relating to disciplinary actions brought against civil servants for the plenary meeting of the higher council. A rapporteur and a chairperson are chosen within each committee at every sitting.

The rapporteur, it must be emphasized, has power to investigate within the departments concerned. He has to look for, with equal attention, what can favour the incriminated State employee and what can confirm the charges laid against him.

The rapporteur acts in the interest of truth : he is neither the accused civil servant's lawyer, nor that of the administration. He has a duty to enlighten objectively.

The rapporteur produces a report at the end of the investigation. The higher council has a deadline of six (6) months within which to give its opinion. The civil servant has at least two (2) months within which to petition the Prime minister after the pronouncement of the disputed decision.

The duties of members of the higher council are free. However, members of the aforementioned council may aspire to sitting allowances as well as to the reimbursement of their transport and outstation expenses following their meetings.

A special decree determines the amount of the sitting allowance.

The new instrument specifies neither the place of the session which was statutorily Yaoundé, nor the freedom the council had to independently draw up its own internal regulations. The council, the new version of the council no longer enjoys the right to subpoena appropriate authorities to hear them nor to co-opt rapporteurs in an advisory capacity in order to facilitate its task as adviser to Government authorities.

b. An advisory organ of the Government

The higher council of the public service functions as a simple advisory organ to government authorities. It was under the minister in charge of the public service. Today it is under the Prime minister head of government, surrounded with a certain number of heads of ministerial departments.

Mr. Eyebe Ayissi in his excellent study on consultative[1] administration underlines the fact that this council had not functioned and that diverse consultations were organized by the minister of the public service at the time that would not have been examined by this body. An inter-ministerial committee met then at the ministry of the public service consisting of representatives of various technical ministries and in the presence of those of the Prime minister's office, the ministry of employment, the ministry of finance and the ministry of the public service.

Inter-ministerial dialogue therefore prevailed over consultative dialogue within the planned framework for the higher council of the public service at the time.

A comparison can today be made with the French case where a similar organ to the said council, the higher council of the public service consists of twenty eight (28) members representing the administration and the most representative of the labour unions. It is also chaired by the French Prime minister. It enjoys considerable moral authority by dint of the skills represented, associated with the effectiveness of the representativeness of the trade union representatives. It coordinates the work of the joint administrative committees, gives opinions, makes suggestions and intervenes as authority of recourse in disciplinary matters, a remit today recognized for the higher council of the cameroonian public service.

---

[1] Refer to EYEBE AYISSI, « L'administration consultative du Cameroun », Mémoire de Masters Degree de Droit public, Faculté de Droit et des Sciences Economiques, Yaoundé, pp. 116-121.

Refer to article 86 of the general rules and regulations of the public service in 2004 ; decree n° 2000/698 of 13 september on the organization and functioning of the Highest council of the public service.

III.2.2- Joint Administrative Boards

A joint administrative board is set up within every corps (article 88 of the general rules and regulations of the public service). In the past, it should be noted, a single joint administrative board common to several income brackets could be established, when the staff of one or several income brackets were insufficient. Boards were joint organs with multifunctional competence. The instruments have today evolved.

a. Boards with equal composition

Every corps has a joint administrative board comprising representatives of the administration and an equal number of representatives of civil servants elected in numbers proportional to the size of the electorate of each income bracket. Formerly, staff representatives of civil servants were elected within each income bracket or group of income brackets by class in a single round single candidate majority ballot. For three (03) years, this election, entirely democratic and self-managed, is moderated by the subsequent appointment of members by order of the minister in charge of the public service.

The mandate of the staff representatives at the joint administrative boards can be shortened or extended for a duration not exceeding two (02) years by order of the minister in charge of the public service, and this in case of necessity of service.

Every class in an income bracket constitutes an electoral college with one full representative and an alternate representative for every ten (10) workers in this class, without the number of elected representatives exceeding twenty (20) therefore, ten (10) full representatives and ten (10) alternate.

A civil servant of the ministry in charge of the public service assumes the secretariat and has no voting rights.

Every joint commission has a president, representing the minister of the public service, members, a representative of the user minister of the civil servant involved, two (02) staff representatives chosen among the elected members.

b. Multipurpose commissions

In the recent past, the joint administrative boards exercised multi-form attributions. They were multipurpose : qualification commissions ; promotions committees to draw up the promotions schedules and propose the promotion of permanent staff ; disciplinary council to give its opinion on disciplinary files established in view of maintaining, the dismissals commission for maintaining or forfeiting the rights to pension for dismissed civil servants ; discharge commission to give its opinion on the opportunity of discharging civil servants as a result of invalidity and on examination of the medical file or in case of professional incapacity.

The current general rules and regulations of the public service are more precise and concrete. They state that the joint administrative board gives an opinion on individual decisions concerning members of the corps within which it is established, especially in matters of promotion in rank, granting of the awards (merit, certificate of excellence and honorary distinction) and of dismissal for irreversible physical inability that is incompatible with the job position, for professional incapacity proven by the results of his evaluation, following special texts that provide for reorganization of services entailing job cuts without possibility of redeployment of the staff.

The joint administrative board meets to decide either on the granting of awards or on dismissals depending on the nature of the matter brought before it.

In conclusion, the power of the joint administrative boards will depend to a large extent on the representativeness of civil servant staff representatives and of the diversification of their labour union membership.

III.2.3- Health boards

The general rules and regulations of the public service (article 86) establish health boards as organs for management of health. A special text determines their organization and functioning[1]. They are set up under the minister for public health.

A National health board meets in Yaoundé and regional health boards meet in the regional headquarters. They are necessarily consulted by the minister in charge of the public service on all medical problems relating to prolonged leaves, to the reinstatement of civil servants after the aforementioned prolonged leaves, to the physical or mental capacity

[1] Decree n° 2000/686/PM of 13 september 2000 on the organization and functioning of Health boards.

required for admission into or maintenance in the public service. They can be consulted for sick leaves not exceeding six (06) months.

a. Attributions of the regional health boards

The regional health boards examine, in first resort, cases of illness that entail a less-than-six-months leave ; cases of presumption of the illness put forth by the civil servant absent from work for periods below or equal to six (06) months ; cases of industrial accident and occupation related illness and applications for medical evacuation within the national territory.

They are consulted, according to the cases, by the user minister of the civil servant involved or by the governor of the region, to whom they send the result of their deliberations.

They are technical and consultative organs of decision-making support.

Besides, the finance minister refers requests for reimbursement of medical bills to the health board with jurisdiction.

The notice is given to every authority, at the level of the regional or national health board.

b. Attributions of the national health board

The national health board is the supreme organ for technical decisions relating to the administrative medical files of civil servants.

It examines in the last resort results of the assessment of the regional councils.

The national health board is necessarily consulted by the ministry in charge of the public service for medical problems concerning :

- mental or physical capacity required for access of workers into or their maintenance in the public service ;

- prolonged sick leave and the reinstatement of the civil servants at the end of the said leave ;

- cases of presumption of illness put forth by the civil servants absent from work for periods above six (06) months ;

- requests for medical evacuation abroad.

The national health board has the power to invite the regional board members to express opinions on certain cases of illnesses requiring a leave of less than six (06) months and cases of presumption of illness put forth by the civil servant who has been absent from work.

Only the gravity of the medical problems to be examined at every level can make the distinction between the attributions of the national health board and the regional health boards.

It would be interesting each time to know the import of the opinion of these technical consultative organs : opinion acceptable or unacceptable.

The main features of the cameroonian public service can be summed up in three points :

i) management structures appear centralized and deriving from the nature of the presidential system of government established by the Constitution of 2nd june 1972, with its several amendments[1]. Despite the creation of the post of Prime minister, this trend has been largely maintained ;

ii) today, the decisive role of the Prime minister and minister of public service and heads of the other ministerial departments (basic education, secondary education, health) who are equipped with a number of useful management prerogatives should be noted ;

iii) it should finally be noted that the principle of authority characterizes the general scheme of these structures, now increasingly tempered by the welcome assertion of certain democratic principles : enjoyment of civil liberties, election of staff representatives, and non-recording of extra-professional observations in the personal records of public officials. The principles of "good governance" and "accountability" have strengthened the penetration of democratic principles.

[1] Refer to OLINGA (A.D), *La constitution de la République du Cameroun*, Editions terre africaine, Presses de l'UCAC, 2006, 326 pages.

CHAPTER II

THE DIVERSITY OF GOVERNMENT PERSONNEL

Broadly defined, diversity was the watchword that characterized the heterogeneous origins and legal situations of government personnel or staff entering into professional relationships with the administration.

A first distinction must be drawn between the staff whose relationship with the administration is not continuous and occasional collaborators connected more tangibly with the administration.

Another fundamental distinction is between staff whose status is contractual and some how precarious and staff with permanent status.

In short, there is a crucial distinction between public officials falling under a special status of the common labour law and government employees subject to the ordinary common labour law. What status therefore should be assigned to those who come into occasional working relationships with the administration ?

I. TEMPORARY STAFF : Casual employees

Casual employees are not part of the permanent staff of the administration. Nonetheless, they still are in a relationship of relative stability with the administration. They lend **voluntary or forced** support to administrative authorities in the performance of some public duties.

The category of employees of the administration is itself heterogeneous and depends on the circumstances of the collaboration.

I.1- The voluntary collaborators with the administration

Voluntary collaborators with the administration are traditionally defined as people who lend support to administrative authorities voluntarily and spontaneously to perform a task of public interest[1]. This also implies the consent or non-opposition of the administration to the collaboration.

---

[1] Refer to AUBY (J.M.) et DUCOS ADER Robert, *Droit administratif*, (2) 3e édition, p. 20.

The examples of collaboration cited by doctrine seem many :

- free and consented participation without requisition, of a person in the fight against fire ;

- de facto management in case of necessity or exceptional circumstances of a public utility, particularly of a municipality ;

- collaboration with public services to track down a criminal (CE april 17, 1953 Pingue R. 177D-1954.7 Morange note) ;

- spontaneous rescue of a drowning person by a passer by (CE march 31, 1957, Cie Urbaine. R 200).

French administrative case law, which may in future affect Cameroonian case law, attaches serious consequences to the voluntary collaboration with the Administration :

i) it extends professional risk allowances and flawless responsibility - liability to voluntary, collaboration ; (CE november 22, 1946 Village of Saint-Priest la plaine R. 245 : requested collaboration to fight fire together by sounding the alarm) ;

ii) it guarantees the third-party - constituent or private individual - against damage arising from a voluntary collaboration by accepting liability of the Administration by the application of the **theory of the de facto civil servant** which validates, just as for regular administrative acts, the acts of the volunteer collaborator (CE march 5, 1948 Marion R. 113).

The legal status of the voluntary worker remains precarious, almost entirely guaranteed by case law alone, without the support of a statutory warranty similar to the guarantees of the civil servant.

Administrative case law retains under normal circumstances the idea of appearance : it is assumed, as underlined by Mr Joseph Binyoum, that the civil servant *in the eyes of citizens is a regular officer*, vested with the powers he has exercised[1] : ruling n° 224/CCA of march 27, 1953 Mrs CIVRA versus Territorial administration. In extraordinary times, our administrative judge retains the idea of necessity of public services. Acts performed by de facto staff are thus deemed valid : ruling n° 4CFJ/ASS

---

[1] BINYOUM Joseph, *Droit administratif*, 2e année Licence (sans date), Université de Yaoundé, p.53.

PI. of november 4, 1965, Mrs Kieffer Marguerite versus State of Cameroon.

"Whereas the self-defence groups were formed with the tacit approval of the Mayor of Nkongsamba and the SDO of Mungo to supplement the inadequacies of the services of law and order ... That the author of this accident, who was sentenced for manslaughter by the Criminal Court of Nkongsamba, must therefore be regarded as having been on duty at the material time and that the case law involving de facto officials must find its application here."

The voluntary collaborator is not part of the staff of the Administration. The apparent membership of the voluntary collaborator on the staff of the Administration could be disproved, thus eliminating any protective "status" granted by case law.

I.2- Workers requisitioned by the administration

The requisitioned workers, as opposed to the voluntary collaborator, is defined as a person compelled by a measure of authority, usually under penalty of law, to cooperate in managing a public service for a limited time and without pay, by a unilateral administrative act ignoring both the consent of the provider and his agreement on the consideration for the services. Any male cameroonian above eighteen years of age may be requisitioned to be used temporarily or permanently in the interest of the nation, in government or endeavours of general interest or contribute directly in defence. Cameroonian women over eighteen years may not be requisitioned in certain branches of the defence services in relation to their fitness or professional abilities for tasks that fall within their usual occupation.

Retired persons up to the age of sixty enjoying retirement pension may also be requisitioned.

The right of requisition is open *ipso facto* by the decree establishing the warning, the state of emergency, partial or general mobilization, and the state of exception. Requisition provides for a mere subsistence, almost symbolic and excluding any possibility of a career. The requisitioned employee receives at most travel and subsistence allowance.

French administrative law recognizes two types of requisitioned collaboration :

- that of times of war or international tension (acts of july 3, 1877, from july 11, 1938, Order of January 6, 1959, Department of labour of the Vichy government) ;

- that of peacetime (national service).

And cameroonian law knows some traditional forms of requisitioned cooperation : jurors and assessors of criminal courts, experts requisitioned by the judicial authorities and witnesses in court[1] that form the category of people conscripted by justice. Law No. 68/LF4 june 1968 authorizes conscription. Police commissioners, officers and commanders of the gendarmerie brigades may requisition individuals and necessary resources in the event of natural disasters or serious accidents. This provision reminds of section 97 of the code of the French local authority that authorizes the mayor to conscript individuals to fight fires.

The conscript is entitled to "**fair compensation**", but incurs heavy fines and imprisonment in case of refusal to comply with the requisition.

I.3- OTHER COLLABORATION SITUATIONS

Other situations of collaboration with the cameroonian administration arise : that of the contract worker with the administration and that of officer of a legal profession.

I.3.1- Contracting parties

The cameroonian government has to conclude many contracts with private individuals (under public or private law) to carry out its many tasks.

The contracting party worker works with the administration on the basis of a contract for the provision of defined services or equipment.

The contract may involve management by an individual of a utility under a concession. The situation of the contracting party, precarious as a result of the exorbitant prerogatives of the administration vis-à-vis him, is far from statutory as that of the civil servant ; even so it is reinforced by the principle of financial equation, financial equilibrium of the contract, which is fraught with fiats of unforeseen constraints.

---

[1] Refer to Cameroonian penal code, articles 173 to 175, pp.173-174.

I.3.2- Officials of the legal profession

The law officials involved in the delivery of public services are excluded from the staff of the administration. They are at the service of the public in the field of justice : notaries, bailiffs, stockbrokers, auctioneers.

Lawyers in Cameroon seem to be in the same situation. They assist and represent parties in court, solicit, claim, plead and give legal advice. They carry out procedural deeds or instruments effecting constitution, transfer, containment or extinguishing personal rights, over real or landed property. They pursue the execution of court decisions, including beginning and following up extra court proceedings, receiving payments and giving receipts. The conditions of access to the legal profession are the following :

i) of cameroonian nationality and enjoy full civil and political rights ;

ii) be at least 23 years of age ;

iii) be a holder of a first degree in law or bachelor of laws, final bar examination or an equivalent diploma recognized by the legal authority and approved by the minister of justice and keeper of seals ;

iv) show proof of good character ;

v) produce a certificate of training or the Post Final Certificate of the Bar ;

vi) be enrolled at the bar set by law.

Without being civil servants, lawyers should be allowed to set up practice by decree of the president of the Republic, after their admission into the bar.

II. GOVERNMENT WORKERS UNDER THE LABOUR CODE OR "CONTRACT WORKERS"

These workers are not subject to the general rules and regulations of the public service. A special enactment (decree n° 72/DF of february 28, 1972) established the legal regime of State officials under the labour code[1], otherwise referred to as workers of the administration or contract workers.

---

[1] See respectively :

- decree n° 74/138 of february 18, article 2.

A complex body of texts now governs the status of state employees under the labour code, creating a special regime, especially subject to the vagaries of the labour contract.

II.1- A NEW CATEGORY : STATE WORKERS OPERATING UNDER THE LABOUR CODE

Before 1972, the category of Government officials subject to the provisions of the labour code and private law in general, appeared composite and heterogeneous. Decree n° 78/484 of 9 november 1978 laying down common rules applicable to State employees under the Labour code came to strengthen the movement to standardize the Decree n° 72/DF/110 of 28 february which created the single category of "*public sector workers*."

II.1.1- The composite category of contract workers before 1972

This category of contractual State employees included both daily-paid Government workers and actual contract employees of the State.

a. Daily-paid government workers (labourers)

The daily-paid workers (labourers) were the subordinate staff of the administration. They received a monthly salary prorated to the number of days of work and provided for under expenditure on material in the budgets of various central and local services. The labourers were recruited by decision of the heads of these services within existing budgetary resources and had a more precarious position than the actual contract workers. These workers, numbering 16,500 in the 1971-1972, fiscal year, were however different from conventional staff used as domestic servants in the various palaces of the State in Yaoundé.

b. "Contract workers" per se

This category included three levels of personnel :

i) Ordinary contract workers, subject to the provisions of the collective agreement for public works, building construction and industry

---

- Decree n° 94/199 of october 7, 1994 establishing the general rules and regulations, amended and completed by decree n° 2000/287 of october12, 2000, article 10.
- And also :
    - law n° 74/14 of november 27, 1974 establishing the labour code ;
    - law n° 92/007 of april 14, 1992.

by order n° 5050 of july 24, 1956 governing relations between employers and employees in the private sector ;

ii) Salaried contract workers, they had the same job classification as civil servants, enjoying the same benefits but not entitled to pension. Their eventual integration into the civil service gave rise to a retroactive reconstruction of their careers. They were mostly teachers recruited by the ministry of education ;

iii) *Contract workers with a fixed wage* ; they were State employees with high professional qualifications who held positions as programmers and translators at the presidency of the Republic, generally with post-graduate training. Their salaries were comparatively higher.

The actual contract workers and the labourers who made up the former category of contract staff of the state are now refereed to as public sector workers.

II.1.2- The category of State employees under the labour code

On 28 february 1972, decree n° 72/DF/110 instituted a single category of contract workers : state workers were assimilated to a large extent to the private sector workers. These workers were hired on contract. Decree n° 78/484 of november 9, 1978 repealed the previous enactment and reformed the labour regime for state employees under the labour code. Law n° 92/007 of 14 august 1992 is the new labour code. These workers were recruited in the following cases :

- for non-permanent jobs or jobs in such small numbers that it was not advisable to create a corps of civil servants to fill them ;

- when the recruitment of staff concerned may, for practical reasons, not obey the rules of recruitment of civil servants as defined by the general rules and regulations of the public service ;

- for tasks requiring high-tech degrees or titles that cannot be classified in those categories defined by the general rules and regulations ;

- for largely subordinate jobs such as house helps, drivers, labourers and guards.

Due to service reeds these rules could be waived on authorization of the secretary general of the presidency of the Republic. Requests for authorization must include a profile of the jobs available and the full list of proposed candidates for recruitment.

The occupational classification of employment of State workers under the labour code included twelve categories of twelve rungs each. The classification of a worker in a category was based on the certificate he held (article 17 of decree). However, the worker who in addition to his certificate had, previous work experience or competence, could receive a bonus in echelon or categories. The transition of a worker in service from one category to a higher could only result from the change of qualification in a trade, justified by the submission of new officially recognized degrees or certificates. It took into consideration the existence of a budget allocation whose introduction may not be deferred beyond the year following the current one.

Decrees n° 72/110 of 28 february 1972 and n° 78/484 of 9 november 1978 had, in unifying the category of contract workers, **sanctioned previous case law solutions**.

Thus the Supreme court of East Cameroon had seen in ruling n° 16 of december 29, 1964 (*Bulletin of Judgments of the Supreme Court p.949)*, that a certain Messina Eboule hired by administrative decision as a fire-fighter to the minister of transport, mines, posts and telecommunications of the Federal Republic of Cameroon was not a civil servant as the workers appointed in permanent jobs of a public administration ; the labour tribunal was therefore competent to adjudicate upon the private contractual dispute, in which as employee, he was an opponent to the State. The Supreme court, in a subsequent Ruling of *15 february 1966*, Henri William Mondoh (bulletin of judgments p. 1389), had also applied the common labour law to a contract worker, simply taking into account the fact that, without being a civil servant, this person had committed his professional activity for remuneration under the direction of another person who happens to be the state[1].

The interest of this case law is today enshrined in the assimilation by an enactment for State workers to private sector workers. Does this assimilation also apply when it comes to recruitment ?

---

[1] Also refer to order n° 23 Supreme court, social chamber : BESSALA Léonard versus the State of Cameroon, 1971.

II.2- THE RECRUITMENT OF STATE WORKERS

The recruitment of State employees is extremely flexible : no formality of the selection methods, no age limit, just the requirement of some conditions similar to those of access to the Public Service, and submission of the applicant to a probation period.

II.2.1- General conditions of employment

A candidate for a job as a state worker must be of cameroonian nationality. The text does not specify whether the requirement of nationality is from birth or whether there is any probationary period after which the naturalized individual may apply for a job in this category. An express derogation from the nationality requirement, provided in case of *impossibility* of recruiting a citizen for special duty, may authorize the hiring of foreign nationals in case of lack of applications from nationals for an offer of employment.

Applicants must be of good character and have not been sentenced to a term of imprisonment exceeding six months for a felony, probity misdemeanour (theft, forgery, influence peddling, fraud, corruption, misappropriation of public funds, breach of trust) or any other sentence with one of the disqualifications set out in paragraphs 1 and 6 of article 30 of the cameroonian penal code. Only an amnesty or pardon can afford to waive this overriding condition. He must not have been subject to an administrative measure of house arrest or confinement for a continuous period of at least five years before from a previous job of any government department or para-statal.

He must meet the physical requirements for the particular job and be recognized, following an examination by a Government medical officer, free from any tubercular, cancer, leprosy, poliomyelitis or nervous disease.

It is prohibited for State and para-statal companies to recruit a worker who was dismissed from a job in the public administration, a State company or a semi-public within five years after his dismissal.

It is arguable that performance of military service, a formality prescribed by presidential decree of 17 october 1972 establishing a two-year compulsory military service "for candidates for any public service," is not required of applicants for employment as State workers, since they are not required to permanently become part of the administrative corps of the State.

II.2.2- Absence of a formal mode of recruitment

"An employment contract is defined, preferably in writing, as... any agreement, contract, decision or other administrative action taking place between *the Administration and a person*, whereby the latter undertakes to put *his professional abilities at the service of the Administration against remuneration*." Article 2 of decree n° 78/484 of november 9, 1978 *does not impose any precise mode of recruitment in respect of public sector workers*. It is to be contrasted with section 54 of the general rules and regulations of the public service, which establishes competitive exams or by qualification as the primary mode of recruitment. There is therefore no predetermined way of selection, leaving wide latitude to those departments needing to hire a public sector worker[1].

However, a purely informal procedure is becoming institutionalized. The department involved determines the need for recruitment ; it launches a job offer through the press and/or radio, stating the conditions required of applicants. They submit applications on time. The administrative authority, ***freely and independently***, selects the candidates considered most suitable and sends their dossiers to the ministry of the public service. This government department draws up the contract for the employees recruited under ***category VII to category XII***, verifying compliance with the classification of the degree or level of training of the staff member concerned. Accounting services of the ministry of finance put their visa on the contract that is sent to the employer ***for final acceptance or rejection***. Consent is evidenced by affixing his signature on the space provided on the contract instrument. Beforehand, the minister in charge of employment issues will have affixed his visa.

Some labour contracts, such as those stipulating a period exceeding three months, or requiring the installation of a worker outside his residence or those involving a worker of foreign nationality, must be established in writing after medical examination of the applicant, and initialled by the national manpower and employment service of the ministry of labour.

---

[1] Refer to article 2 of decree n° 72/110 of february 28, 1972.

These final formalities do not reduce the flexible nature of the recruitment process of public sector workers : the ministry of finance only verifies the regularity of the act of employment with respect to budgetary provisions (decision or contract) and the ministry of the public service, the regularity of the worker's job classification. ***The freedom to choice of the administrative authority responsible for the recruitment remains free and total***, even at the risk of loading the administration with old people into this category of State agents under the labour code.

The "contractualization" of the temporary workers carried out during the last half of 2008 confirms the extra flexibility of this recruitment procedure for which the requirements were :

- to have been recruited latest june 16, 2006 ;

- to have been identified in 2007 ;

- to be as of 1st january 2008, 17 years of age at least and 45 years at most for workers employed by decision and 50 years at most for contract workers ;

- to have a genuine recruitment certificate ;

- to hold a deed of employment as a temporary worker signed by an administrative official (decision, memo, list, contract, agreement) ;

- be of Cameroonian nationality[1] ;

- must not to be serving in an organization with autonomy in management (mutual benefit society, project, management committee).

II.2.3- Absence of the age requirement

The regulations in force do not insist on an age requirement for recruitment of public sector workers. Article 51 of the rules and regulations of the public service is more rigorous : the age limit for recruitment of civil servants is set *between 17 years and less than 35 years for jobs in categories B and A, at least 17 years and 30 years at most for jobs in categories D and C.* A special instrument sets the age limit for admission into retirement of civil servants for each corps. The civil servant may not be kept in service beyond this age limit. The lack of

---

[1] Source MINFOPRA, october 2008.
OLAMA ONGBWA (F.), *Le guide des formalités administratives et juridiques du Cameroun*, p. 82.

an age limit for recruitment of state workers beards to increasing *stay-at-homes* of a *number of civil servants eligible for retirement* in this category.

However, it can be stated that the provisions of **article 93 of the labour code** prohibiting the employment of children under fourteen remain in force here.

An application of the regulatory text concerning **State** employees on the rules and regulations of the public service would contribute to the rejuvenation of this category of personnel.

II.2.4- The submission of applicants to a probation period

State workers are hired individually by **decision** for workers in **categories I to VI** and **on contract** for **categories VII to XII**. This act spells out the usual references : identity (name, sex, date of birth, nationality) place of recruitment, place of employment, occupational category, level, salary of the worker hired.

Any worker engaged under these conditions is subject to a probationary period in accordance with the regulations in force. The probation shall be made in writing in the contract or decision.

The labour code sets the maximum period of probation at six (6) months, except for supervisory staff and executives for which this period may be renewed for a similar period. This period should correspond strictly to the length of time required to test probation of the applicant. A special text of 1968 reduced this period to fifteen days for labourers, one month for domestic staff and two months for other employees.

II.3- A CONTRACTUAL LABOUR REGIME

The labour regime for State employees is essentially contractual, reinforced by the legal stipulations of the Labour Code and the regulatory provisions of the decree of november 9, 1978. These provisions organize the worker's career in the administration, determine his benefits and clarify his obligations without in any way diminishing contractual hazards.

II.3.1- The State Worker's Career

The state worker performs a real career ; jobs are classified, he is promoted and helps manage his career.

a. Job classification of State workers

The occupational classification of jobs for State workers has twelve categories divided into **twelve grades** each. A minimum wage is indexed to each grade of each category. The classification of the worker in a category depends on the certificate he holds. The transition from one category to a higher one can only result from the change of qualification justified by the submission of new degrees or certificates officially recognized this is subject to budgetary allocation and its inclusion can not in any event, be deferred beyond the year following that year.

A worker who, after his recruitment, comes up with a degree or certificate higher than that which warranted his classification in a category but not usable in the professional specialty in which he works, cannot rely on it to qualify for reclassification.

In exceptional cases, subject to the corresponding budgetary allocation and the 1% limit of workers fulfilling the requirement, the workers whose manner of serving has regularly been satisfactory may, upon proposal of the joint committee responsible for advancement, be promoted to the next higher category if they :

- have exhausted all levels of their category ;

- have at least ten years of experience in this category ;

- have scored over the last three years of service an average of performance grades at least equal to the stated minimum.

A worker may receive such a reclassification only once in his career.

b. Advancement of workers

A state worker is employed at the first grade of classification in their category. The worker laid off for down-sizing purpose and reintegrated at the same category maintains the benefits of the grade reached during the layoff. Advancement in grade takes place every two years. It takes into account both the workers length of service and his proper way of serving annually, evidenced by a mark sheet. The minimum score requirement for professional advancement is 17/20. The shift to a higher echelon is automatic and as of right after four years ; an unsatisfactory score may delay the advancement for one or two years. Advancement is recognized by decision of the head of the ministerial department after consulting the joint committee for advancement. A satisfactory budget allocation for the progress of workers is provided annually by each jurisdiction concerned. The latter is bound to do so.

c. The participation of the state employee in the management of his career

Each ministerial department has a joint committee with jurisdiction over advancement.

The committee decides on the basis of annual mark-sheets and appraisals. The advancement proposals of the committee are submitted for decision, first to the head of the department involved with regard to workers employed by decision for categories I to VI and, secondly, to the minister of the public service regarding contract employees for categories VII to XII under his management.

Every worker has the right to ask the administration to check if the category to which he belongs corresponds to his professional qualifications. He may send his request directly or through a staff representative who shall submit it to the competent authority, who will review it taking into consideration the terms of his contract.

d. The uncertainties of the state worker's contractual condition

The state agent in several aspects can be likened to the worker in the private sector :

- working time is 40 hours per week and 173 hours per month ;

- he has two working days of paid leave for full continuous or discontinuous work periods of five years in the Department ;

- special permission may be granted for family events touching his own home, under the following circumstances and conditions : **three days** for the worker's wedding, **three days** for the death of his father, mother, spouse or a child, **three days** for the birth of the worker's wife, **one day** for the marriage of a child.

Totalling about ten days a year, these permissions are not subject to any deduction from the wages for monthly paid workers. To workers paid on an hourly basis, they are considered as "hours actually put in" on duty for the duration of the permission. These periods may be extended if the event occurs outside the town of employment and requires travel. Travel expenses shall be borne by the worker in all cases. However, the contractual condition exposes the State worker to hazards.

e. Suspension of the employment contract

A distinction should here be made between industrial accidents and occupational illnesses, on the one hand, and accidents and illnesses not attributable to the workplace, on the other.

Industrial accidents and occupational illnesses come within the competence of legislative and regulatory provisions common to Labour Law. In such cases, the Authority takes care of the medical, surgical, pharmaceutical and funeral expenses and transportation of mortal remains and the possible admission of the victim into a State hospital until recovery. In cases where the worker cannot resume his previous job after consolidation of his condition, the Administration assigns him tasks corresponding to his new physical abilities.

Absences justified by disability resulting from an illness or accident not attributable to work suspend the employment contract for a period of six months. This period is extended until the recovery of the worker. During the suspension period, the worker is subject to a precarious allowance system. His compensation is equal to one month's salary if he has already put in less than twelve months' of duty, two months salary for a period of duty equal to or greater than five years. The duration of duty includes paid holidays, paid or unpaid special leaves, and periods of contract suspension under Article 6 of the Labour Code.

f. Breach of the contract of employment

The employment contract of indefinite duration may still be terminated unilaterally by one party, behoving such party to observe the notice to be given to the other party.

The worker loses the right to notice and severance pay in case of dismissal for serious misconduct, subject to the assessment of the characterization of the fault.

He cannot claim any salary for unauthorized absence for whatever duration. The worker who has received notification of his employment decision or has accepted and signed his contract and refuses to report to his post at the first request of the administration, is deemed to have resigned and de facto breached his contract. It is noteworthy, emphasizing the randomness of his contractual situation, that the general rules and regulations of the public service (article 156) require a written resignation marking an unequivocal decision of the civil servant to finally leave the corps to which he belongs.

In case of dismissal, the administration shall forward its notification of termination by a decision indicating the amount of wages and allowances accruing to the worker upon termination of services.

The employee dismissed, in case of breach by the administration, of a contract of indefinite duration, is entitled to a redundancy allowance separate from the notice. However, the dismissal should not be motivated by gross negligence of the worker and the latter must have completed at the time of termination at least two years of continuous service in the Administration. The statement of allowances obeying fixed rules defined by decree n° 78/484 : damages are calculated.

- 20% of the total average monthly salary for each of the first five years ;

- 25% of the same amount for the period between the sixth and tenth years ;

- 30% of the same amount for the period beyond the tenth year.

II.3.2- Benefits of State Workers

The State worker is first entitled to pay. Other benefits are granted him by the State.

a. The salary of State Employees

The public sector worker is entitled to a salary which may be accompanied by accessories :

a.1- The wages of public sector worker

Wages are stipulated to be paid monthly except in the case of staff recruited for a period of less than a month, which are paid on an hourly or task basis. The hourly wage is obtained by dividing the salary of the worker for over a month. It is less well protected than the salaries of civil servants : the attachable portion is greater.

It should be stressed that the principle of compensation for services after they have been rendered is the only one applicable : hence the importance of an attestation of assumption of duty.

a.2- Eventual allowances

The State official is entitled to certain benefits.

There is first of all displacement allowance. When a worker is displaced, the regulations establishing the system of displacement of civil servants and civilian officials of the State is applied. Unless where the terms of individual contracts are more favourable, the worker is entitled to transportation expenses for himself, his family and his luggage from the administration.

Housing is provided to the worker in the cases and conditions stipulated by the laws and regulations. In case of breach of the employment contract, the worker lodged in a house provided by the Administration is obliged to vacate. In the case of breach of contract by the worker vacation is immediate, and the prior notice period is not respected. A one work deadline is given, upon the worker's request, if the employee is dismissed by the administration. And the vacation takes place at the expiration of the notice period where prior notification was done on time.

Moreover, the public sector worker who occupies a position of high administrative responsibility is entitled to various constraint allowances attached thereto, if any.

b. Other benefits

The general labour law and decree n° 78/484 grants a number of benefits to state workers.

i) The right to syndication : article 3 of decree n° 78/484 of 9 november 1978 provides that the right to syndicate is guaranteed to workers under the laws and regulations.

They elect staff representatives following the system established by the labour code.

ii) The right to family allowances : family allowances granted to government workers mostly consist of birth allowances (prenatal and maternity allowance), family allowances and a daily maternity allowance is paid for women with at least six consecutive months of work during the period of maternity.

iii) The right to paid leave and compassionate leave is also guaranteed

iv) The right to protection against occupational hazards

In case of occupational illness or industrial accident, government takes care of medical, surgical, pharmaceutical and funeral expenses and transportation of mortal remains and the hospitalization in a State health facility until recovery or mending the state of the victim.

v) The right to funeral benefits

In case of death of a worker, government provides the coffin to his family. If the worker was displaced because of the Administration, it also assumes the transportation of the corpse from the place of death to the place of residence provided that the family requests it. It is the same for the mortal remains within a maximum of two years after the statutory deadline (of the contract of employment). Wages and all benefits earned at death pass of right to his heirs (spouse, legitimate children, illegitimate children recognized before death, foster children).

II.3.3- The obligations of the State worker

With a few exceptions, the state worker is subject to public service obligations comparable to those of the civil servant.

a. Professional obligations of the public sector worker

Article 10 of decree n° 78/484 of 9 november 1978 binds the public sector worker to several professional obligations.

a.1- The obligation to devote himself to his work.

The State employee owes his professional activity to the government on whose behalf he was recruited. Does the scope of such an obligation include the worker's exclusive dedication to her of his professional activity alone as determined in the contract ? The regulatory instrument here is less rigorous than the general rules and regulations of the public service (articles 47 and 48) that create an obligation "to provide service and devote himself," and enacts express prohibitions of activity. Decree n° 77-504 of 15 december 1977 strengthened this requirement by prohibiting the exercise of lucrative activity for some state officials and staff of public institutions and para-statals.

"*It is prohibited for State employees* :

i) *"To have, under whatever description, whether by themselves or through intermediaries, any interest, either in a business dealing directly or indirectly with the State, or in a sector under their direct control or in relationship with them, either in a public or para-public company with state participation,*

ii) *"To carry out personally or by proxy, a private money-making activity"*

This prohibition does not apply to farming and pastoral activity, to the production of scientific, literary or artistic works, or to part-time teaching. Moreover, when the spouse of a public official is engaged in a private profit making business, this must be declared by the worker to the minister under whom he works. This statement is made to the manager who will inform the appropriate minister in the case of a worker or an executive of a public company or a mixed enterprise company.

a.2- The obligation to protect Government interests

The worker must refrain from any activity likely to prejudice his service. He is required to protect the interests and image of his administration.

a.3- The obligation to professional secrecy

The public sector worker is bound by professional secrecy. He must not disclose or let show outside his service, neither facts, written documents, nor information to which he may be privy in the course of his duty.

a.4- The obligation to loyalty

Decree n° 78/484 subjects the public sector worker to the obligation of loyalty as an employee. Note should be taken of the more political rather than legal character of this requirement in the cameroonian context, a political system guided by strong ethical imperatives of development and nation building. However, the courts must assess the scope and substance of this duty of loyalty just like for the civil servant.

b. The disciplinary action over these obligations

The disciplinary procedure for the State employee is more expeditious, compared to that in force for the civil servant.

Any breach of professional obligations entails, the following sanctions, depending on the severity of the misconduct : warning, reprimand, 1 to 8 days suspension, delay in promotion of 1 to 2 years, grade demotion, dismissal. These sanctions are in order of severity. The warning, reprimand and suspension are made by the hierarchical authority vested with the power to discipline. The other penalties may be imposed only by the authority with powers of recruitment. Sanctions are always justified and notified in writing. The last four sanctions are subject to a decision. Suspension is also subject to the prescriptions of the labour code.

The State worker, except in the case of a final conviction, shall be allowed to justify himself. To this end, once the fault is found, a query should be served on the individual.

Dismissal for gross misconduct entails for the state employee the loss of rights to notice and severance pay. The act of abandoning his duty post amounts to gross misconduct ; this introduces a sharp distinction between State agents, public sector workers under the labour code and public officials of the State even without a permanent status.

III.3.4- Public employees without a permanent status

Three types of public employees without permanent status exist in the public service : interns, assistants and members of ministerial cabinets.

a. Probationers

They are public officials seeking eligibility for a permanent status within one of the ranks of the civil service. They are compelled to prove their professional competence, good character and fitness to perform the functions to which they aspire. The probation term is one year of actual service. Students of some training schools are considered as probationers by a text or a special status. A former provision of the general rules and regulations subordinated this presumption to two conditions : the school located in Cameroon or abroad would necessarily serve to recruit for some permanent jobs in the administration and students had to receive a salary from the budget of Cameroon.

A probationer enjoys the rights and obligations of the civil servant with permanent status. Probation is mandatory for any candidate for Public Service. It should last one year of effective service and may be extended only once for an equal period if unsatisfactory. It may not exceed two years. However, special rules and regulations and laws governing training schools can consider the duration of the course to be probation.

Probation ends, either in tenure, which confirms the probationer his job, or by dismissal. Disciplinary proceedings during the prescribed period of probation suspend the tenure process. The grounds for dismissal of a "civil servant on probation" fall within the sovereign power of the Administration : Ruling n° 15A Ekwalle Eyango Edoubey Stéphane *versus* the Federated State of East Cameroon, april 25, 1974.

b. Administration auxiliaries and daily-paid workers

Originally, this was a class of workers recruited within the limits of the staff budget for temporary occupations and not organized in income brackets. In France, various texts (decree of april 19, 1946, and decree of 29 september, 1950) gave them guarantees and organized them into income brackets : the administrative judge is competent for disputes concerning them, possibility of gaining permanent status and regulation of the dismissal procedure.

In Cameroon, antiquated[1] texts clarified the course of their careers and benefits of the corps. The labour code refers to special provisions applicable[2] to them and excludes them from its sphere of competence.

b.1-The career of a government auxiliary

It is a career open to former soldiers, and labourers in the private sector, who can show proof of two years of professional practice and in priority, for daily-paid workers of the administration who have put in two years of effective duty.

A great proportion of the available jobs (70%) is reserved, for veterans holding a card issued by the office of ex-service men, cameroonian volunteers and retired or active cameroonian soldiers.

Candidates who rigorously must be of cameroonian nationality, must have successfully passed a practical test of professional competence and produce a file obligatorily containing some vital documents : copy of birth certificate, criminal record, medical certificate declaring them fit for the job applied for, a medical certificate from a physiologist designated by the administration, certificate of professional practice, etc.

The status of auxiliaries of the administration has come closer to that of civil servants :

- requirement for a shorter probationary period of six months after which their immediate boss makes a motivated report, transmitted to the authority having power to appoint and who decides ;

[1] Refer to orders n° 343 of july 7, 1955 and 344 of the same date completed by decree 59/21 of 2/14/1959 organizing the corps of administration auxiliaries and order n° 137/CAB/PR of July19, 1971.

[2] Refer to labour code, article 1, paragraph 3.

- selective promotion to the next higher level after two years and with good assessment scores.

The disciplinary system for auxiliaries of the Administration has also jurisdictionalized : requirement of disclosure of the record and providing a written explanation of the facts alleged against him before any sanctions, and prior summoning before a disciplinary board.

b.2- Benefits of auxiliaries of the Administration

Auxiliaries are entitled to paid annual leaves and medical care. They receive remuneration embellished with numerous supplements : special additional pay, weighting allowance for the high cost of living and difficulty of life, family allowance.

They are entitled to an annuity of seniority acquired after twenty years of service and fifty years of age. No one shall be maintained in the auxiliary functions beyond the age of fifty.

Auxiliaries are public officials in the same way as other categories. This category of public workers is being progressively phased out[1].

b.3- Other provisions concerning auxiliaries, daily-paid labourers and domestic workers of the State

An old text (instruction n° 16/CAB/PR of 9 november 1978) also governs the daily-paid workers.

The initiative to create jobs for labourers and auxiliaries in the central and external services of the State and governors' offices, sub-divisional offices, divisional offices and districts offices, is from the ministers acting under the Finance law responsible, for the transfer of a job to the province or changing the legal status of a job.

In preparing the budget, ministers receive proposals from all their services. They appreciate the opportunity to recruit and cause this to reflect in their estimates.

They can include new positions in the regional services concerned or regroup them at the central level under a single budget category ; distribute them by job creation orders in the province or by transfers of budget items.

[1] Refer to TEKAM, *Fonction publique camerounaise, Op cit.*

A ministerial decision or order puts the daily-paid worker or auxiliary at the disposal of the regional authorities.

The minister concerned may proceed in the same way in case of transfer or reassignment of staff in central services.

The change of the legal status of a job is made by an order of the Minister concerned ; for example, transforming an auxiliary job to that of a daily-paid worker or of a civil servant by way of special competitive examination, or of raising a daily-paid job to that of civil servant, hence its disappearance from the range of jobs thus offered.

Daily-paid workers and auxiliaries of the provincial services are managed by governors. They transfer them when duty requires and send copies to the various ministers as a report.

The draft decisions of governors on the recruitment and dismissal are approved by the regional finance department and legal and administrative division of the governor's cabinet.

Circular n° 13/CAB/PR 9 november 1978 regulates the recruitment of domestic staff of the State, assigned to the official homes of members of government and the residences of heads of administrative districts.

The minister of finance was the sole authority to hire and fire the domestic servants in the homes of ministers and of those in the same category on their proposal.

And the minister of territorial administration was alone responsible for the recruitment of staff for the residences of heads of administrative districts.

These recruitment procedures were subject to the approval of the Prime minister.

The circular established a simpler procedure limiting to the sole competence of the ministers concerned, their recruitment within the limits of available budgetary allocation. The recruitment of domestic staff for the residences of administrative authorities reverted to the jurisdiction of governors.

c. Members of ministerial cabinets

In France, members of ministerial cabinets are only considered as public officials when they have the quality of civil servants and where their appointment was properly decided as prescribed by texts.

This solution also applies for the appointment of private secretaries of ministers in Cameroon, who come from diverse backgrounds and owe their positions to the sole trust of their minister. The ministerial cabinets themselves have been deleted in the cameroonian government departments, cadres par excellence for the employment of civil servants per se[1].

III. CIVIL SERVANTS OR TENURED PUBLIC OFFICIALS

Statutory enactments and case law precisely discern the actual concept of civil servant.

III.1- CIVIL SERVANTS AS PER ENACTMENTS

A distinction must be drawn between the civil servant as defined by the general rules and regulations of the public service and the civil servant by predetermination of the law.

III.1.1- A civil servant as defined by of the Rules and Regulations

"Shall be deemed to be a civil servant within the meaning of paragraph 1 of Article 3 of the general rules and regulations of the public service, any person holding a permanent job and is tenured in a hierarchy of the administration of the State[2]*"*

This article is a simple remake of the previous text (paragraph 2 of article 2 of the general rules and regulations) [3].

The definition adopted compares the French legislation of the ordinance of 4 february 1959[4] with the cameroonian regulation of the federation period[1].

---

[1] See MVONDO Jérôme, « Le chef du Secrétariat particulier dans l'Administration Camerounaise », Mémoire de Licence 1977-1978, Droit public, 67 pages.

[2] Decree n° 94/199 of october 7, 1994 establishing the general rules and regulations of the public service of the state, amended and completed by decree n° 2000/287 of october 12, 2000.

[3] See above decree n° 74/138 of february 11, 1974 on the general rules and Regulations.

[4] Compare to :

1° Order of february 4, 1959 defining civil servants in France as persons appointed in a permanent job, later tenured in some grade of the hierarchy of the State central administrations, external services or either dependent thereof, or public institutions.

2° Decree n° 66/DF/153 of february 13, 1966 : (Cameroon) « Agents titularisés dans un des cadres de hiérarchie de l'Administration fédérale créés pour l'exercice des compétences définies aux articles 5 et 6 de la Constitution de 1961 ».

The civil servant, vis-à-vis the administration, is in a statutory and regulatory situation. In France the situation is regulatory and statutory.

The duty post, with prior provision in the State budget, is the set of tasks, duties and responsibilities requiring special knowledge and skills. Any civil servant may change their duty post within one or more departments.

The corps is made up of all civil servants with a specific function in a sector of activity and governed by the same regulations[2].

III.1.2- The Civil Servant by predetermination of the law

Criminal law (article 131 of the cameroonian penal code) provides a broader definition of the civil servant :

"For the purposes of this code, any public official, or person who even occasionally is charged with a public service or mission, any magistrate, officer or non-commissioned officer of the armed forces, any officer of the gendarmerie force acting in the exercise of his functions[3] *shall be considered a civil servant. Specific texts organizing certain training institutions for senior executives of the administration, may assign the status of civil servant*[4] *by predetermination."*

III.2- THE CIVIL SERVANT AS PER CASE LAW

How does case law define the civil servant ? Does it rely only on statutory elements ?

Cameroonian administrative case law recognizes the status of civil servant only for individuals belonging to a part of the Administration into which they were incorporated (CFJ october 16, 1968, judgement n° 9 State of Cameroon versus Baba Youssoufa).

In so doing it is only following the footsteps of the French administrative courts, particularly the Council of State (CE. 20 december 1946 Colony of Madagascar D 1947.464) and the disputes tribunal (CT march 28, 1955 Laborde P. 618) which at times see :

---

[1] Ibid.
[2] Ibid.
[3] Ibid.
[4] See the cases of national administration schools.

"A worker entrusted with a permanent job within a public utility, and at another a worker appointed into a permanent job within a public administration[1] *".*

This case law has seen some progress in the number of rulings and in precision referring to a civil servant who died while on official assignment, as "civil servant on secondment[2].

III.3- ELEMENTS FOR A DEFINITION OF CIVIL SERVANT

In the light of enactments and case law, the status of civil servant has several components.

III.3.1- Notification / integration

The civil servant is recruited by appointment, that is to say by taking a unilateral administrative act ; in contrast, the State worker governed under the Labour Code is recruited into a category by indenture (bilateral act) or by decision establishing his recruitment. Can we admit recruitment by word of mouth as in the famous case of "Mr and Mrs Bertin" ?

III.3.2- Permanent employment

The status of civil servant presupposes occupation of a permanent duty post, that is to say a permanent job (CF march 24, 1905 Vautron D.308). Provision for the duty post is made beforehand in the state budget and "*corresponds to the set of tasks, duties and responsibilities requiring special knowledge and skills.*" This causes us to exclude from this category tenured public employees, workers on part-time employment and assistants to the administration.

III.3.3- Tenure in a rank of State hierarchy

Tenure is the formal legal process of integration of the interested person into the hierarchy of a specific corps of the administration of the State. It confers the status of civil servant.

Besides, the latter, for that purpose, is assigned a matricule number which be used throughout his career.

---

[1] See MVONDO Jérôme, « Le chef du secrétariat particulier dans l'administration camerounaise », Mémoire de Licence 1977-1978, Droit public, 67 pages.
[2] Ibid.

Tenure intervenes after a successful probation during which the Administration is able to assess the civil servant's professional abilities, physical fitness as well as morality. It opens the door to the career of civil servant.

It should therefore be noted that the civil servant exists only in the administrative hierarchies of the State excluding other organs. Local councils, para-statal and public industrial and commercial establishments do not on their own employ civil servants. Until now, only the State intended to use civil servants.

However, the laws on decentralization enacted in 2004 already suggest the creation of local public services with local civil servants who can pursue a career similar to that of tenured public employees[1] in the hierarchy of the State administration.

---

[1] Refer to law n°2004/17of july 22, 2004 on the orientation of the decentralization ;
- law n° 2004/18 of july 22, 2004 fixing rules applicable to communes ;
- law n° 2004/19 of july 22, 2004 fixing rules applicable to regions.

CHAPTER III

THE CIVIL SERVANT'S CAREER

Specific rules predetermine the stages of a civil servant's career : entry, progress and termination thereof.

I. RECRUITMENT OF THE CIVIL SERVANT

A general principle dominates access to the public service : the principle of equal entitlement to public employment. General conditions of access are predetermined and the competitive examination remains the main method of recruitment.

I.1- THE PRINCIPLE OF EQUAL ENTITLEMENT TO PUBLIC JOBS

The principle of equal entitlement to public jobs for all citizens is rooted originally in article 6 of the Declaration of human and citizens rights 1789 :

"All citizens are equally eligible to all public jobs without distinction except that of their abilities and talents."

This rule in France constitutes a general principle of Republican law and was confirmed by affirmative law, primarily by a provision in the preamble of the 1958 Constitution. In Cameroon, the June 2, 1972 Constitution does not state it explicitly. However, this principle can be regarded as being an affirmative legal rule by the reference in the preamble to the civil liberties enshrined in the universal declaration of human rights that the cameroonian State "guarantees citizens.[1]" The constitutionality of the principle of equal entitlement to public employment can therefore be reasonably asserted without fear of contradiction.

Consequently, all citizens have access to the public service if they meet the general requirements for access to the specified category.

---

[1] See article XXI 2° of the said declaration : « Toute personne a droit à accéder dans les conditions d'égalité aux fonctions publiques de son pays ».

Stigmatization is not allowed in the public service and certain public offices cannot be closed to some citizens.

Do statutory enactments and case law recognize what the Constitution so solemnly guarantees ?

The general rules and regulations of the public service are unequivocal. They stipulate :

"Access to the public service is open without discrimination to any person of cameroonian nationality fulfilling the requirements subject to constraints specific to each corps.[1]*"*

It would be interesting to compare this with the old formulation of article 5 of the former general rules and regulations : the reserve of "physical fitness" and that of the inherent requirements of certain jobs specified by the special rules and regulations.

The said general rules and regulations tie separate recruitment to the opinion of the higher council of the public service when the situation of the applicant is a crucial precondition for access to the public service.

It is the same where distinctions can be made to take inability to hold certain jobs into account.

France recruits on a sex basis where sex is an essential condition for the exercise of functions[2].

French administrative case law (CF, 28 may 1954 Barel 1959 504, quashing the expulsion of a communist candidate from the entrance examination into ENA) is implicitly followed by the administrative bench of the Supreme court in Cameroon sanctioning the positivness of equal entitlement (CFJ ruling 9 of 18 october 1967, in the suit Joseph Peck Peke versus State of Cameroon). French public law on the public service recognizes the principle of equal access. The exclusion of members of families that reigned over France may still exist for the post of the President of the French Republic.

[1] Refer to article 12 of the general rules and regulations, decree n° 94/199 of 10/7/1994.
[2] Article 21 of the general rules and regulations of the French public service, Title II.

I.2- RESTRAINTS ON THE PRINCIPLE OF EQUAL ELIGIBILITY

In France, the principle of equal eligibility currently has few restrictions :

relative restriction on the principle of secularity of the State that prohibits access to primary education for clerics : the State council has extended this exclusion to secondary education (CE may 10, 1912 Abbot Bouteyre) ;

- sector-specific restrictions on "reserved jobs" considered as compensation for ex-service men included on a ranking list.

In Cameroon, express statutory exceptions have tended to disappear under the onslaught of liberalization and good governance.

I.2.1-The decline and reduction of expressly statutory exceptions

a. Disappearance of the exception for senior leadership

The exception for senior leadership has disappeared from the general rules and regulations. In the past, article 16 of the general rules and regulations, then in force, provided an exception to certain provisions that :

"Promotion to certain functions of high administrative responsibility is left entirely to the discretion of the government. This promotion is essentially revocable and precarious. It does not confer any vested right and can not allow one's tenure into a rank of the function. "

However, special regulations have waived the mandatory rule thus stated. Paragraph IV of article 13 of the special rules and regulations of the corps of civil servants of the general administration (decree n° 75/774 of 18 december 1975) provided, however, and surprisingly, that senior civil administrators may be chosen outside the personnel of the general administration among persons aged at least 40 years and having exercised for at least ten consecutive years, some features of high political and administrative responsibility in public, parapublic services or in international bodies.

Some special rules and regulations at the time (diplomat) contained such derogations allowing exceptional integration within the highest ranks[1].

The list of functions of high administrative responsibility was determined by a decree of the president of the Republic.

These types of special rules and regulations were ambiguous especially as the practice at the end of Ahidjo's rule (1970/1982) tended towards the exceptional integration of a slew of civil servants in these corps of the general administration and diplomacy[2].

Could special rules and regulations depart from the general rules and regulations and undermine the principle of equal access to public service ?

It should be noted, with satisfaction, that the notion of function of high administrative responsibility has disappeared from the general rules and regulations. The door therefore would seem to have been closed to certain abuses.

It should also be noted that another ambiguous concept, that of duties requiring "loyalty to the institutions of the Republic or absolute political neutrality", of their holders is looming[3]. These would be the subject of a special text still to be enacted. Would it be a "resurrection" of the functions of "high administrative responsibility ?"

b. Maintaining the exception for the position of clerics

The functions of cleric are incompatible with membership of, maintenance in or recruitment into the corps created under the provisions of the rules and regulations of the public service. The question remains whether this exception allows retroactive exclusion of civil servants who discover and respond to their religious calling later[4]. However, clerics contribute to public service missions as contract workers of the administration.

---

[1] See article 10-IV, decree n° 75/773 of December 18, 1975 on the specific status of State agents in the diplomacy.

[2] Ibid.

[3] Refer to article 21 of the general rules and regulations of the public service (decree n° 94/199 of october 7, 1994 and amended texts).

[4] Refer to article 14 of the general rules and regulations of the public service.

One informed observer notes and it is surprising that in practice, many civil servants are religious leaders[1].

The latter exception appears illogical and is incompatible with the constitutionally secular State of Cameroon.

I.2.2- Other exceptions to the principle of equal access

Other exceptions are possible and are worth noting :

i) The exception of physical fitness and the exception of constraints that are specific to certain jobs specified by special regulations are laid down under article 5 of the general rules and regulations. One can here glimpse, shrouded by a discreet veil, the foundations of statutory exemptions relating to sex to exclude the "male proletarian" from certain functions[2].

ii) The exception of "special conditions" exclusive for certain jobs is provided by article 54 of the rules and regulations which suggests the possibility of adding special rules and regulations to the general uniform conditions for all civil servants. There is still the problem of determining the specialty of these conditions : territorial, sectorial or regional specialty ?

Cameroon public law has so far opted for a philosophy of "regional balance"[3]. Order n° 59/70 of 27 november 1959 establishing the general rules and regulations for civil servants proposed a system of admission of natives from under-educated areas in to public jobs. Several enactments have come up dealing with the matter :

- decree n° 61/100 of 21 june 1961 laying down detailed rules for the implementation of order n° 59/70 ;

- order n° 1504 of august 30, 1961 designating the divisions recognized as under-educated (Adamawa, Benue, Diamaré, Logone and chari, Margui wandala, Mayo danaï, Lom and kadey, Upper nyong Boumba and ngoko) ;

---

[1] TEKAM, *Fonction Publique camerounaise, Op cit*, p.12.

[2] See CE 2nd may 1959, Dame VIAUROUX, « La jurisprudence française en la matière ». Also CE 6 June 1956, « Syndicat national du cadre d'Administration générale des colonies : illégalités de l'exclusion automatique des femmes mariées d'une fonction ».

[3] See NKEMEGNI (N.), *Contribution à l'étude de l'équilibre régional au Cameroun*, Thèse Doctorat 3e Cycle Faculté de Droit et Sciences Economiques, 1981.

- addendum n° 556 of october 11, 1962 adding the Bamun division now called the Noun ;

- Order n° 177 of april 8, 1964 retains only divisions of the North as under educated ;

- decree n° 66/DF/339 july 23, 1966 creates a list A reserved for nationals from under-educated areas ;

- decree n° 75/496 of 3rd july, 1975, came to confirm "these reserved positions."

The modalities of the distribution of these places were subsequently carefully spelled out between regions[1] :

Central South	: 19%
East	: 4%
North	: 30%
North West	: 12%
Littoral	: 12%
South West	: 8%
West	: 13%

The Minister in charge of the public service determines by a special instrument the quota of jobs reserved for candidates from each province, given the demographic significance and school enrolment of their home provinces. The province of origin is that of legitimate parents.

I.3- CONDITIONS FOR ACCESS TO PUBLIC EMPLOYMENT

The principle of equal eligibility does not exclude submitting access to public employment to certain uniform conditions for all which are compatible with the principle.

I.3.1- Cameroonian nationality

Access to the civil service requires the possession of cameroonian citizenship.

[1] Refer to order n° 4107 of october 4, 1982.

Article 13 of the current general rules and regulations, disdaining the footsteps of former Article 16 of the rules and regulations of the federal public service, does not foresee the possibility of a career in our public service to citizens of another African State within the framework of cooperation within the organization of african Unity or in cases provided under international agreements. The current cameroonian text does not specify whether cameroonian nationality at birth is the only one required and if it is not required for the naturalized cameroonian to graduate from the five year citizenship course to qualify for the civil service.

I.3.2- Regulatory age requirement

The regulatory age for access into the civil service is strictly determined :

- From at least seventeen (17) years to thirty-five (35) years at most for civil servants in categories A and B ;

- From at least seventeen (17) years to thirty (30) years at most for civil servants in categories C and D.

The applicant for a permanent job in the public service should neither be too young (under 17) nor too old (over 35) for categories B and A, more than 30 years for categories C and D. The administration complies with the international ban on children and is developing a wide range of years of service for staff entering the public service, at least twenty (20) years of service unless exceptional extension of the retirement date.

The Prime minister, upon proposal of the minister in charge of the public service, may extend the statutory age limit for access to a duty post of category A on an individual basis. It is worth remembering that the Prime minister has previously used this discretion very sparingly and cautiously. He has done so for some students graduating from the higher teacher's training college in excess of age and to allow the recruitment of doctors into the civil services corps of penitentiary administration[1].

Moreover, decree n° 67/DF/107 of march 15, 1967 to facilitate the integration of former soldiers into the public sector, allowed the age limit to be rolled back for a duration equal to that of seniority in the armed forces or the police force, but not exceeding five (05) years.

It was a real "decree for services rendered."

---

[1] Refer to TEKAM, *Fonction publique camerounaise, Op cit.*. p. 11.

I.3.3- The requirement of good character

The applicant for access to the public service, should not have had custodial sentence :

- For a *felony or misdemeanor* like theft, forgery, influence peddling, embezzlement, fraud, corruption, misappropriation of public funds or breach of trust ;

- For an offense that resulted in a prison sentence of six months[1]. "

It should be noted that the disqualifications stipulated under article 30 of the penal code are equally applicable in assessing the requirement of good character and the requirement of total integrity of the applicant.

He must not have been victim of any of the following disqualifications :

i) removal and exclusion from all public duties, jobs or offices ;

ii) being unable to be sworn in as an expert assessor or juror ;

iii) being banned from the guardianship, trusteeship, guardianship appointed by a family tribunal or legal advisor except for one's own children ;

iv) ban on wearing any decoration ;

v) prohibition from serving in the armed forces ;

vi) prohibition to run a school or teach at an educational institution or to handle duties relating to education or care.

These disqualifications are not broad and apply only for specific fixed objectives.

In total, one must be of good character to enter the cameroonian civil service.

To avoid any discriminatory and discretionary decision of the Administration, it is imperative that the administrative judge be able to independently interpret the fluctuating concept of good character :

TE Ruling n° 2/6 of september 28, 1961, Tchomgui Elijah.

CFJ/CAY/ november 4, 1966 (Tsala Mekongo Germain).

---

[1] See general rules and regulations, article 13.

I.3.4- Fitness for military training

Candidates for the civil service need to comply with the law on army recruitments and military training.

It should be remembered that a decree of february 2, 1969 69/DF/6 made military training compulsory for students in some vocational schools for civil servants :

- National school of agronomy ;
- National school of administration and magistracy (ENAM) ;
- Higher teacher's training college (ENS) ;
- University centre for health sciences (CUSS) ; and
- National advanced school of engineering (ENSP).

I.4- COMPETITIVE EXAMINATION FOR ACCESS INTO THE PUBLIC SERVICE

The methods of recruitment into the civil service around the world are varied and differ from each other by the degree of freedom allowed the Administration to choose prospective applicants[1].

There are :

- "***Qualification based recruitment***" which takes place without special tests but based on certificates or qualifications of candidates (article 15 of the general rules and regulations of the public service, october 7, 1994), respecting the modalities defined by the specific or special rules and regulations ;

- Election based recruitments *where civil servants are elected*, so as to establish a democratic link between them and the community[2] :

"Administrators are officers elected by the people on time to exercise administrative duties under the supervision and authority of the King," (Title III, chapter IV, section 2, article 2 of the Constitution of 1791).

This method of recruitment proved troublesome since it can not always lead to the popular choice of technically competent individuals. It

---

[1] Refer to KESSLER (M. C.), « Historique du système de formation et de recrutement des hauts fonctionnaires » dans *Revue Française d'administration publique*, n°1, janvier/mars 1977, AP, Paris.
[2] Ibid.

promotes corruption and in Cameroon its practice limited to the selections of the administrative body of the municipality, the mayor[1]. It is in force in the U.S. thanks to the "*Spoil's System"* (spoils) and was practiced in the former USSR.

"***Cooperation***" refers to the process whereby the civil servants in place designate the civil servant of tomorrow. This process is sometimes followed through enabling competitive examinations : eg French aggregation of faculties of law, economics and management and political science. It remains a tough and impenetrable contest ;

"***Venality of office***" consists in the purchase of office by the civil servant. It was abolished for all, in all offices, positions and public employment by the proclamation on the night of august 4, 1789 (article 6 of the declaration of the rights of man and the citizen of august 26, 1789) ;

"A***ppointment***" which is analysed as a unilateral act of investiture by the competent administrative authority on recruiting new staff.

French royal power had established "***tests of ability***," often deemed not serious, to test the knowledge of certain categories of staff notably the future consultants for Parliament. The 1789 register of grievances demanded real competitive examinations.

Today, the competitive examination has become the main method of recruitment of civil servants :

"*Recruiting in the public service is competitive...*" (article 15 of the general rules and regulations 1994) [2].

Recruitment on the basis of qualification is also allowed.

A decree of the Prime minister has set the legal regime for competitive examinations for recruitment[3]. Their aim is to fill the jobs available in the public service. They refer to all modes of recruiting civil servants

---

[1] Refer to article 52 of law n° 74-23 of september 5, 1974 on the organization of communes and subsequent texts, particularly law n° 2004-18 of july 22, 2004 fixing rules applicable to communes (article 60, paragraph 2 : « the Mayor is elected at the single ballot in two turns… »).

[2] Refer to article 54 of the 1974 general rules and regulations.
EDOA EFFA, « Le Concours administratif au Cameroun », Mémoire de Licence Faculté de Droit et des Sciences Economiques, juin 1976, pp. 26-36.

[3] Refer to decree n° 2000/696/PM of september 13, 2000.

consisting of a selection of candidates to fill the available jobs in government departments.

To this end, annual planning and budget allocations based on needs expressed by government departments are drawn up.

A review of the types of competitive exams and the prerogatives of the minister of the public service in organizing them is necessary.

I.4.1- The types of administrative competitive examination

Four types of entrance examinations for the civil service coexist (article 7 of the general rules and regulations) : direct competitive examinations, professional competitive examinations, special competitive examinations and competitive examinations for training scholarship.

a. Direct competitive examinations

They are open to eligible candidates fulfilling the uniform requirements determined by the general rules and regulations and who hold the qualifications required for recruitment into a cadre of the administration.

They are held whenever the number of places offered is higher than that of vacancies.

The civil servant who is already tenured within the public service, who is enrolling for a direct competitive examination for entry into another corps, must obtain the prior approval of the minister in charge of the public service after consultation with the user minister.

It is our opinion that it can be obtained by regularization, because the administration, by allowing his participation, can not avail itself of its own turpitude, which, by parallelism of forms, can be granted retroactively by the user minister and by regularization.

Direct competitive examinations for access to jobs in categories A and B have four papers and two oral tests, one of which is English for French speakers and french for anglophones. Formerly, the written tests were three in number and one of these events could be replaced by a practical test. The language tests, French or English up to 1980 were optional for access to categories A and B.

Practical tests remain optional for these categories.

Direct competitive examinations for access to jobs in categories C and D have three written tests.

Coefficients for tests proposed for direct competitive exams, for categories A and B as well as for categories C and D, are ordered in a descending order 5, 4, 3, 2 and 1 where appropriate. This provision appears not to have always been respected by the administration.

The successful candidate at a direct competitive examination is appointed as from the date of assumption of duty and under the conditions determined by the corresponding rules and regulations.

b. Professional competitive examinations

Professional competitive examinations are open to tenured civil servants, either for promotion to a higher rank within a cadre, or to move to the cadre immediately above.

The age limit for enrolling for professional competitive examinations is fifty (50) years for access to jobs in categories A and B and forty-five (45) years for access to jobs in category C. They were extended surprisingly for a country with a surplus of young people.

Applicants must have put in at least five (05) years of actual service in their rank.

Professional competitive exams for access to jobs in categories A and B have two written papers, one on general knowledge (coefficient 4) and a technical paper (coefficient 6), a language test (coefficient 1) and an oral test (coefficient 1).

The oral test for categories A and B jobs can be replaced by a practical test.

For access to jobs in category C, we have the general knowledge paper (coefficient 4) and a technical paper (coefficient 6).

The professional competitive exam is not the only way forward within the same cadre. One can also change rank through longevity of service. Advancement within the same cadre is steady.

Candidates declared successful at a professional competitive examination are appointed as from the date of publication of the results of that competitive examination.

c. Special competitive examinations

Recruitment into the permanent cadres of the public service may also be done through special competitive examinations open to State employees with status as auxiliaries or under the Labour Code.

The requirements of candidates for a special competitive examination are the same as those imposed and required of candidates for same-level direct competitive examinations, with the exception of that relating to age.

The candidates allowed to compete in such competitive examinations must, have put in at least five (5) years of actual service in the Administration as auxiliaries or State workers under the Labour Code.

For access to categories A and B have two written tests one of which may be substituted with a practical examination and two oral tests including language.

Special competitive examinations for access to categories C and D consist of two written tests.

The distribution of coefficients between tests of the special competitive examinations is the same as the coefficients in professional competitive examinations. These coefficients are 4 for the general knowledge written test, 6 for the second written test and 1 for each of the oral tests.

Successful candidates are appointed as from the date of publication of the results under the conditions set by the corresponding rules and regulations. They have an appropriate monetary compensation.

d. Competitive scholarship examinations

Candidates for competitive scholarship examinations can be either State agents governed under the Labour Code or civil servants exclusively of all other candidates.

These examinations are organized for the selection of candidates for national, foreign or international scholarships for training or further training.

The text launching the competitive scholarship examination defines the conditions to be met by candidates, the nature of the tests and their coefficients.

I.4.2- The prerogatives of the Minister of the Public Service

The Minister of the Public Service is seen as the Minister of competitive examinations except for the organization of entrance examinations into educational institutions that do not train future civil servants and which fall within the competence of the ministers of the said institutions (see decision n° 4/02966/MINESUP/DDES/PEEX of may 17, 2004 for admission into the Faculty of medicine and biomedical sciences).

He is involved at every stage of the organization of such exams : launching, drawing up of the lists of candidates admitted to compete, organization, etc.

a. Launching of competitive examinations

Competitive examinations are launched by administrative orders of the Minister in charge of the Public Service.

He centralizes the staff requirements expressed by the various ministerial departments and establishes an annual schedule of recruitments based on the available budgetary allocations.

The competitive exam should aim at responding to job reeds in the Administration and not recruiting with a social purpose to fight against unemployment or promoting political patronage.

Our opinion is that the jurisdiction of the Minister in charge of the Public Service is total in the launching of competitive examinations for public service recruitments.

He is as such responsible for recruiting into the Public service, successful students of training institutions, which is by direct competitive examination.

The order of the Minister in charge of the Public Service launching the competitive examination specifies its nature and purpose, *the number of places to be competed for*, the examination dates and centres, the list of tests and their time schedule and the requirements for enrolment on the list of candidates.

All administrative competitive examinations must be launched three (03) months before the holding date except in emergencies.

The launching act is publicized. It is made public by way of posters, press publication or insertion into the Official Gazette.

b. Drawing up the list of candidates

The list of candidates allowed to compete is determined by the Minister in charge of the Public Service or on delegation by the regional manager responsible, at least ten days before the date of the tests.

It is made public by posting in the various examination centres.

The publication of the list of eligible candidates serves as notice. It may be followed by individual notices.

The Minister in charge of the public service, before the act, verifies whether the candidates meet the requirements for the competitive examination. He may, after review of records, eliminate candidates who do not meet those requirements.

Applications for competitive examinations are sent to the Minister in charge of the Public Service no later than thirty (30) days before the date of the tests.

Every candidate for a direct competitive examination must produce a file.

This includes several documents :

- A handwritten application for registration of the candidate, ***stamped, dated and signed*** with complete information on the candidate, the competitive examination in question and the choice of tests ;

- A certified copy of the candidate's ***birth certificate or other document in lieu thereof*** ;

- A police record not more than three (03) months old ;

- An attestation of presentation of the original certificate required ;

- A money order or other document confirming ***payment of registration fees*** ;

- A medical certificate of less than three (03) months ;

- An authorization to compete for civil servants.

It should be noted that the Minister in charge of the Public Service shall issue prior authorisation for civil servants tenured within a cadre and wishing to switch cadre by direct competitive examination.

In practice, this authorisation has tended to be granted by regularization.

The constitution of the file may vary depending on the type of administrative competitive examination :

- The recruitment decision is required for a special competitive examination ;

- The integration decision is attached to the stamped application and the money order for registration fees ;

- The authorization to compete is required for internal candidates for competitive scholarship examinations for admission into a national training school.

Candidates for (direct, professional, special) administrative competitive entrance examinations into a national institution must pay a registration fee.

These fees are valid for one enrolment only. Proof of payment of fees is a sine qua non of participation in the examination.

Payment of fees is due at the time of filing the application.

Payment is made to a board created for that purpose in the Ministry in charge of the public service by order of the Minister of Finance.

Registration fees are non-refundable. They are meant to cover organization costs and the modalities are determined by the Minister of Finance and the Minister in charge of the Public Service.

The list published by the Minister in charge of the Public Service may be contested. A candidate can only be excluded for reasons of public interest. Every one has a right to compete. There is no discretionary power to exclude undesirable candidates[1].

Acceptance to compete creates rights, mainly the right to take part in the competitive examination and the right to equal treatment with other candidates. Illegal rejection may bring legal action against the Administration (Case Barel EC. May 28, 1954 conclusion Letourneur R. 208). And the judge may want to know the reasons for the refusal (CE december 21, 1960 Serra and Vicat Blanc D 1961. Chapus 421 note).

---

[1] Refer to French law :

VLAVAU, « Le prétendu pouvoir discrétionnaire d'exclure un candidat d'un concours », JCP, 1953 I. 1128.

DABEZIES, « Le problème du droit à concourir », RDP, 1967. 1133.

Any candidate who, uses **false** or **forged documents** for the constitution of his application file for an administrative competitive examination, is excluded from that examination.

He shall also be **banned from applying for a competitive examination** for a period of four (4) years. The measure is taken by order of the Minister in charge of the Public Service.

The candidate at fault also incurs criminal or disciplinary sanctions.

c. The organization and conduct of tests

The Minister in charge of the public service has general responsibility for organizing purely administrative competitive examinations[1].

1. The Minister in charge of the public service chooses the topics of the tests upon the proposal of the head of department involved or any other expert. There is a question bank in the ministry in charge of the public service.

The questions selected must be conform with the topics defined in the order launching of the competitive examination.

Question papers are sent on time to the heads of the invigilation centres by the Minister.

The question papers for each test and for each centre are sealed in an envelope. The envelope bears the name of the centre, the purpose of the competitive examination, the nature of the test and the date and time of its holding.

The envelopes containing the various questions of the same examination for each centre are packaged in a sealed and stamped envelope and addressed to the head of the supervision committee.

The latter, on receipt of the parcel, in the presence of the other members of the supervision committee, opens it and ensures it contains all the necessary envelopes.

In the case of any shortage, he should immediately refer to the Minister in charge of the Public Service to claim the missing question papers.

---

[1] Refer to article 23 of decree n° 2000/96/PM of september 2000 ruling the general system of competitive examinations.

The sealed envelopes containing the question papers shall only be opened in the examination hall.

A report on the opening of the parcel shall be drawn up and signed by *all members of the Invigilation Committee present*.

2. The Minister in charge of the Public Service sets up a committee for the supervision of the written tests at the examination centres opened. This committee may, by delegation, be constituted by the Governor or by the Senior Divisional Officer upon proposal of the local Public Service official.

The head of the diplomatic or consular mission with territorial jurisdiction shall set up a supervision committee in examination centres located outside Cameroon.

The Minister in charge of the Public Service or his representative chairs the supervision committee of the Yaoundé centre. Regional and divisional delegates play the same role in their constituencies and the cultural attaché or advisor plays the same role abroad.

3. The Minister in charge of the public service ensures the general discipline in the conduct of the examination through the supervision Committee.

The supervision committee checks the presence of the candidates and the conformity of the information on their identity cards with the one written on the lists of candidates authorized to compete. Candidates must come along with their official identification documents.

The head of the supervision committee invites the candidates already ushered into the examination hall, to get rid of any unauthorized document in their possession.

After the installation of candidates, he opens the sealed envelope containing the question papers.

The starting and closing time of the test is made known to the candidates.

Candidates who come late are not allowed into the examination hall after the envelopes have been opened.

No candidate is allowed to move out of the examination hall without completing the answering and handing over his answer sheet, unless he is accompanied by an invigilator.

Questions are answered on a special answer sheet supplied by the Administration.

Candidates' answer sheets are rendered anonymous by the supervision invigilation committee immediately after the end of the tests.

They are forwarded under sealed, stamped and signed parcels addressed to the Minister in charge of the Public Service by the members of the invigilation committee.

This parcel must also contain the reception report of the tests as well as the invigilation report.

4. The Minister of Public service is the addressee of invigilation reports and of reports of *duly* established fraud.

A fraud is in effect established in a statement signed by the President of the supervision committee of the examination centre. Invigilators in charge of the hall do also sign, as well as the defrauder who must countersign. In case of refusal, mention is made of this on his behalf.

Documents possibly seized from him are clipped on his script. The mention "excluded for fraud" is written on the roll of candidates.

The introduction of unauthorized documents into the examination hall is considered as an attempt at fraud, even if they have no connection with the test questions.

Furthermore, candidates are forbidden, under penalty of disqualification, to sign or make any marks and signs likely to disclose their identity on the answer sheets.

The decision to expel candidates caught in the act of committing fraud or who disrupt the progress of the test is taken by the supervision committee that decides by a simple majority of the votes. In case of a tie, that of the chairperson prevails.

Finally, it should be noted that the supervision committee is responsible for any irregularity in the conduct of the examination ; especially one to which the attention of the minister of public service as not been drawn to, in the invigilation[1] report.

---

[1] Refer to article 41 of decree n° 2000/696/PM of September 13, 2000 ruling the general system of administrative competitive examinations.

d. Marking of written tests

The marking of written tests is done in a secure room by a committee whose president and members are appointed by the minister in charge of the public service.

Registrars maintain the answer sheets anonymous.

A **second marking** may be ordered by the minister in charge of the public service's competitive examinations. It has become a rule for candidates aspiring to enter category A.

e. Compilation

The Minister of the Public service sets up a compilation commission.

It is composed of a representative of the Minister of Public service who acts as president, a representative of every ministerial department interested in the examination as member, one or several workers of the Ministry of Public service to assume the secretarial without the right to vote. Markers can be part of the compilation commission.

This commission goes through the scripts recording the scores obtained by each candidate on a review form. They also calculate the total marks obtained by each candidate in all the written tests, and then rank candidates by order of merit.

Candidates ranked in the order of merit are recorded in a report which is forwarded to the minister of public service, who then draws up the results according to the number of vacancies in contest.

The compilation report is signed by the chairperson and the members of the committee.

f. Oral tests

Once programmed, oral tests take place before a jury set up by the minister of public service.

This jury includes a representative of the minister (president), persons selected by the Minister by dint of their competence as members, then one or several workers of the ministry in charge of competitive examinations to ensure secretarial duties without a right to vote or take part in the decisions.

Members of the jury must hold a rank at least equal to the one to which the candidates aspire.

The jury for oral tests stands as the jury for admission.

This jury records the scores obtained by the candidates at the oral tests in an interview form. It adds these scores to those obtained in the written or practical tests.

The jury submits the list of candidates ranked in the order of merit to the Minister in charge of civil service examinations on a record signed by its members.

g. Qualification for orals and final admission of candidates

A candidate qualifies for orals when he has totalled up to an average of at least **ten over twenty (10/20)**. Nobody qualifies with an eliminatory mark.

Whatever the case, qualification for orals in one cannot be carried over to another session of the examination.

The total marks of the oral tests are added to those of the written part.

The candidate finally admitted is the one who has scored at least **twelve over twenty (12/20)**.from all the tests of the competitive examination. The number of places offered must be taken into account.

Admission automatically becomes void thirty (30) days after the beginning of the course for competitive scholarship exams, forty five (45) days after publication of the results for direct competitive examinations.

It must be emphasized that any person recruited as a civil servant on the basis of fraudulent manoeuvres during a civil service examination "*is dismissed* " by the authority with powers of appointment without prejudice to any legal action and civil proceedings which may be brought against him.

h. Other prerogatives of the Minister

The Minister in charge of the Public service has other prerogatives in matters of civil service examinations.

He may issue to any candidate a transcript of the scores obtained in the various tests.

Waiting lists, by order of merit, may be drawn up for candidates who obtained the minimum total of points required, but were not retained, as a result of the restricted number of places offered.

Candidates on the waiting list must have obtained the required average. The former option where in the Minister of Public service could step down the minimum average has been revoked. To be declared admitted the candidate must score a total average of 12 over 20 or above.

Through a decision the Minister of Public service may, depending on the case cancel, the results of the candidate or all the candidates proven guilty of fraud in the afore mentioned competitive examination.

He may cancel the competitive examination itself, in case of blatant violation of the principles governing the organisation of civil service examinations.

I.4.3- Interventions of the Prime Minister

The Prime Minister, Head of Government issues a decree on the allowances to be allocated to members of the various supervision, marking, compilation committees, and members of the admission jury. This decree is yet to be published.

In the meantime decree n° 90/1086 of june 15th, 1990 still governs the system.

The allowance allocation is as follows : fifty thousand (50,000 CFAF) for the chair of a competitive examination, thirty thousand (30,000 CFAF) for a committee chair, and one thousand five hundred (1,500 CFAF) for a half-day invigilation or participation in compilation.

The marking fee rate is three hundred francs (300 CFAF) per script for level A examinations, a hundred and fifty francs (150 CFAF) for level C and hundred francs (100 CFAF) for level D.

The rate of payment for a half-day as jury member of the orals Committee is three thousand francs (3000 FCFA) for level A, two thousands (2000 FCFA) for level B, and one thousand for level C.

The Prime Minister, Head of Government is also empowered with deciding the quota of places reserved for the candidates from each region of Cameroon.

The candidate's region of origin is the one from which his father or, mother originates.

The application of this statutory quota does not exempt candidates from obtaining the required averages of 10 over 20 for qualification, and 12 on 20 for admission.

The abovementioned text determines quotas as follows :

East	: 4%
Adamawa	: 5%
South	: 5%
North	: 7%
South-West	: 8%
North-West	: 12%
Littoral	: 12%
West	: 13%
Centre	: 15%
Far North	: 18%

The distribution into regional quotas takes into consideration the population and levels of school attendance of the region.

It has become common practice to group regions into pools when a region is unable to provide the number of places allocated cannot :

Pool1 : Adamawa, North and Far North ;

Pool2 : Centre, South and East ;

Pool3 : Littoral and the West ;

Pool4 : Northwest and Southwest.

A candidate who is successful at a competitive examination is assimilated into a cadre and gets a permanent job with the Government.

He then begins his career as a civil servant involving the various stages, rules for promotion and statutory positions.

II. CAREER EVOLUTION OF CIVIL SERVANTS

After probation, the candidate admitted in the competitive examination is integrated into the public service, which means he is appointed civil servant in a permanent job position within the administration hierarchy. His career can thus start and evolve following the various stages ; his progress is based on his turnover and what assessment is made of him.

II.1- PROBATIONAL INTERNSHIP FOR THE CIVIL SERVANT

A compulsory internship is prior to any absorption into the Public service : "*any newly recruited civil servant shall undergo probation...*" (article 19-paragraph 1).

II.1.1- The notion of internship

The candidate deemed apt by the compilation commission is proposed for admission. The competent authority declares the candidate admitted by publishing his name on an admissions' list.

He is going to carry out administrative duties during a temporary and probationary period of one year of effective service. Probation is a period of observation during which the civil servant admitted in a competitive examination, who should be given tenure in an employment or permanent job, has to prove his professional value, good morals and physical capacity to ensure the duties to which he aspires.

As such the trainee should not be judged on extra statutory criteria as political militancy or religious beliefs.

The judgement must be founded on good morality, professional ability to assume the functions in question and on his professional skills.

Is the probation compulsory ? As stipulated in the current rules and regulations which adopt the former phraseology of article 24 of the former general rules and regulations of the Public service, notwithstanding the exceptions provided under the private rules and regulations, clearly enunciating the principle of a preliminary compulsory internship for any appointment on a permanent basis to a salaried employment by the federal Public service : " *any newly recruited civil servant shall undergo probation*" (article 19, 1st paragraph of the 1994 general rules and regulations of the public service).

We should however note that special rules and regulations authorize dispensations.

A special instrument, decree n° 116 / PM of march 27th, 2001, lays down the legal status of Government probationers and probation conditions[1].

An original aspect of this instrument is that it gives consideration to a particular category of probationers : "*the civil servant who in the course of his career is successful at a professional competitive examination*" granting access to a senior rank.

His status seems quite ambivalent :

- He is subject both to the regulations in force on training courses and to those of the special rules and regulations of the corps from which he originated ;

- He is subjected to the provisions of the general rules and regulations and, if admitted into a training school as a student, to those governing the said school.

At the end of the training course, he may be appointed on a permanent basis, while preserving his seniority or access to an upper grade. Ordinary trainees usually start as beginners at the first grade level.

In the special rules and regulations and texts governing training schools, the training period can be assimilated to the probationary internship. It is then probation by assimilation, by predetermination of the rules or of the law.

II.1.2- Legal regime of the probation

1. The probation lasts one year effectively. It may be extended for an equal period once, in case of unsatisfactory results. It must be a period of continuous effective service.

However, a trainee may be forced to repeat the course all over if he was ill for a period of up to 6 six months within the twelve (12) months course. The same applies for a female trainee who, at the expiration of her maternity leave, is not apt to resume service.

Can the "*ad hoc committee*" have a future civil servant, repeat a training course by reason of his poor results ? It is not expressly prohibited by the regulations. It should be noted that the general rules and

[1] Refer to article 19 of the 1994 General rules and regulations of the public service 1994.

regulations clearly provide for a training course of no more than one year, whereas the application text grants only two (02) express exceptions which are : the case of the six-months sick worker and of the woman who, is unable to resume work after her maternity leave.

2. What is the legal status of a trainee who has not yet been appointed on a permanent basis in a grade and permanent position in the Public service ?

Let us note that generally the " trainee civil servant" (an ambiguous expression), recently successful at a competitive examination is subjected to the terms of the general rules and regulations of the public service (art 4 of the decree n° 200 / 116 / PM of march 27th, 2001).

Is he subjected to the special rules and regulations of the corps of civil servants he wishes to be part of ?

In some cases, students of training schools through which the recruitment of some civil servants is done, are during the training period, governed by the rules and regulations of these schools.

The "trainee civil servant" cannot, in this capacity, be put on secondment or on temporary leave of absence.

The trainee nevertheless enjoys the same rights as permanent civil servants as regards vacation : administrative annual leave, sick or maternity leave.

He is subjected to the same regime of special authorizations and permissions.

We should finally bear in mind that he is subjected to the disciplinary regime applicable to civil servants.

However, the range of disciplinary measures a trainee may encounter is not wide : they are restricted to first warning, final official warning and dismissal.

The dismissal of a trainee for misconduct is proclaimed by the authority invested with the power of appointment after consultation with the permanent disciplinary council of the public service.

Sanctions like first and last official warnings are meted out by the following competent authorities : Secretaries general of ministries, directors of the central administration, senior divisional officers, divisional officers and regional delegates.

What happens to a trainee if the internship was unsatisfactory ?

In that case the latter is dismissed after the opinion of an "*ad hoc* committee" set up and chaired by the Minister of public service.

Other cases of dismissal may occur :

- Lay off for physical unfitness or disability on the advice of the Health Board. The laid off worker is given a disability pension if his disability was as a result of duty. In that case, the Administration also takes care of the medical and hospitalization expenses under the same conditions as for permanent civil servants who became disabled in the course of duty ;

- The dismissal at any time for acts committed before admission to the training course, which could have obstructed his recruitment, if they had been known to the Administration. This time the "*ad hoc* committee" is not consulted and the dismissal may occur at any time...

The dismissal of a "trainee state employee" is pronounced by the authority vested with the power to make appointments.

We should note that the motives for laying off a trainee are left to the sovereign power of the Government. His appointment on a permanent basis or integration depends on the discretionary – not arbitrary- powers of the Administration in accordance with legal principles and relevant regulations (Ruling n° 15 of April 25th, 1974 FJ/AP Ekwalla Edoubey Stéphane versus the State of Cameroon). This decree cancels the integration decision of the aforesaid within the cadre of agricultural supervision. The latter was dismissed after twenty seven months of training for his “usual poor manner of serving”[1]. Besides, he did not have the required certificates, that is, a diploma from the Cameroonian National School of Agriculture or from a higher school of rural engineering and forestry, recognized equivalent.

The interested party was rightfully no suited.

The dismissed trainee is not entitled to receive any lay-off allowance. However, all the deductions made on his wages for the constitution of his pension benefits can be reimbursed in totality.

---

[1] Refer to « Cour suprême du Cameroun – Répertoire chronologique de la jurisprudence de la Cour suprême Droit Administratif », 1ère partie, par DIPANDA MOUELLE Alexis, p.67.

Besides he is also entitled to get free transport for himself and his family from the place of service to the usual residence, under the same conditions as for civil servants on final departure.

There is nonetheless a peculiarity : the dismissal of a civil servant who became trainee in view of acceding into another cadre automatically warrants his reintegration to his previous cadre if his internship proved unsuccessful.

Can he be reintegrated in case of dismissal for indiscipline or incompetence ?

That would be utterly illogical especially in a matter of blatant lack of probity or incompetence.

The training also ends in case of resignation or death of the trainee.

If the training course was conclusive, the agent is appointed on a permanent basis in his job. The appointment is decided by the Minister of public service, starting from the end of the normal period of training.

The trainee must have had a favourable assessment. The applicable regime is that of decree n° 2001/108/PM of march 20th, 2001 indicating the modalities for the assessment of civil servants.

i) The civil servant admitted in a training school is assessed according to the rules and regulations in force in the school.

ii) The assessment of trainees and civil servants alike is based on the results obtained following objectives defined by the hierarchy, as well as norms established by every administration : enumeration of tasks and assessment of objectives.

We can affirm that for civil servant trainees, certain qualities are essential in their assessment : professional knowledge ; managerial skills, sense of public duty, organizational and methodical ability, conscientiousness, rapidity in the execution of work, punctuality and assiduity, public relationship and relations with the hierarchy... These are the most significant professional qualities and personality attributes.

The year of the internship is considered achieved at the first rank, when calculating seniority for the promotion of the future tenured civil servant.

However, a trainee having served as a civil servant in another cadre of the Public service is treated under a favourable scheme.

He can be reclassified at the same, or the next higher grade compared to the one he had in his former cadre, in case of a lower initial index provided in the new private rules and regulations under which he now falls.

In case of appointment with an equal index he maintains his seniority, acquired in his former cadre. Above 30 points, seniority is cancelled.

A positive point about the new general rules and regulations (1994) is that they clearly define the status of a civil servant admitted into internship for access to another cadre.

A normal and satisfactory end of internship means an appointment on a permanent basis into a rank and a permanent job in the Government.

II.2- APPOINTMENT OF CIVIL SERVANTS ON A PERMANENT BASIS

The appointment on a permanent basis incorporates the civil servant into a hierarchical structure of the State administration. It places the civil servant in a **statutory and regulatory position**, different from that of employee under contract. It ties him to a permanent job and connects him with a corps of civil servants with specific duties in a determined sector among the public sectors.

Currently in Cameroon we speak of integration and recruitment on a permanent basis whereas French law uses the term : appointment.

Integration or appointment on a permanent basis is subjected to rules in their form and content. It produces specific effects.

In Cameroon the appointment on a permanent basis is pronounced by the Head of State following the provisions of particular or special regulations.

In some other cases, the Prime minister was delegated in the past, in most cases, to integrate and appoint civil servants on a permanent basis.

II.2.1- Conditions for the validity of appointments on a permanent basis

Five (05) conditions seem to govern the system of integrations or appointments on a permanent basis :

1. The Procedure follows particular rules : the publication and submission for the visa of the financial controller.

The visa is required for the new job position to be inserted in the Government budget. To this effect, the Minister of public service closes the annual budgetary endowments established according to the recruitments needs.

In the past there was an administrative visa by the services of the presidency of the Republic. The extension of the competences of the Prime minister may explain why it is no more used.

The visa of the financial controller has a major aspect.

2. Motive is another condition. There must be a vacant post to be provided for. However, it does not mean that a vacancy in a corps must be imperatively filled. This explains the invalidity of supernumerary appointments, and the real need to publish job vacancies when launching competitive examinations.

3. Purpose is another condition. Appointment on a permanent basis must be aimed at legitimately filling vacant jobs. Appointments by order, entailing a theoretical appointment to a post, are invalid. Article 15 of the former general rules and regulations forbade any appointment or promotion exclusively aimed at filling a vacancy.

4. Objective of the appointment must thus be regular, since any appointment entails the application of a status to an individual that is a set of pre-existing rules.

The act of appointment must not be arbitrary. The competent authority is bound by the order of presentation of the candidates by the jury, which is the compilation commission. He cannot appoint just anyone. He can order the opening of another competitive examination. He can refuse to appoint candidates for previous acts that are in compatible with belonging to a corps of civil servants.

5. "The exercise of jurisdiction" of **appointment on a permanent basis "over time"** is also retained. The administration, that is the authority endowed with the power of appointment, has to follow the rules of jurisdiction *ratione temporis*. Some appointments are considered illegal :

- retroactive integrations having come into effect in the past. Case law accepts cases of career reconstruction up to the result of the competitive examination ;

- anticipated integrations which cannot concern the future ;

- promises of appointments on a permanent basis which can engage the State's responsibility, invalid with regards to the law. (February 24th, 1956 Leduc RPDA 1956.62).

That is why the 1994 general rules and regulations clearly enunciate the following rule : "the corresponding appointments come into effect as from the date of assumption of duty ".

Any appointment on a permanent tenure in a permanent job of the Administration and any admission at a competitive examination or into a training school, occurring in violation of these conditions, can be revoked at any time.

II.2.2- Effects of tenure (appointment on a permanent basis)

We should be able to distinguish between the effects of regular integrations and irregular integrations.

a. Effects of regular integration

A regular appointment on a permanent basis confers the quality of "civil servant", entailing the integration of the person concerned into a corps, with predetermined rules laying down his rights and duties.

It is a major act/ condition for the career of the civil servant.

This career begins with the permanent appointment of the person concerned, so that he now has to formally and definitively report to the hierarchy of a corps of the government.

The appointed person is installed. The ceremony includes the establishment of a certificate of assumption of duty. This enables to state that the interested person has taken up duty at his duty post.

b. The effects of irregular integration

The integration or irregular appointment can result in disqualification in due form. The Administration can retroactively revoke the appointment, from the day of the irregular appointment.

Such termination of an irregular appointment can give rise to a dispute, requiring a decision of the administrative judge. Decree n° 15 of april 25th Ekwalla Edoubey Stéphane against the state of Cameroon (report of the Supreme Court cases 1st part p. 67) illustrates this assertion.

Mr. Ekwalla's integration was annulled by the Supreme Court.

French law should have to admit, the disqualification of irregular appointments very restrictively. Only appointments on order may be disqualified at any time (june 30th, 1950 Massonaud R.400).

On the contrary, the 1994 general rules and regulations of the cameroonian public services are clear and precise this matter :

« Notwithstanding any criminal and civil proceedings which may be instituted against him, any person recruited as a civil servant through established fraudulent means shall, as soon as such fraud is uncovered, be dismissed from the public service by the authority with powers of appointment" (article 58).

The defrauder may be dismissed at any time and his integration revoked.

Appeals may be filed by candidates who deem they were entitled to be integrated in the same corps, for example those who were proposed by the compilation commission in order of merit.

In French administrative law, the judge refuses, in the interest of citizens, to cancel acts carried out by sanctioned civil servants, by having the notion of appearance and de facto civil servant prevail (IT n° 1923 Association of civil servants of PTTR.699).

II.3- POSITIONS OF CIVIL SERVANTS

There can be several types of situations in the administration, which we call "the positions of civil servant "namely : active service, on secondment and on release.

Cameroon does not recognize secondment, a usual position in the French public service, in which a civil servant stops benefiting from his salary, advancement and pension rights and is no more subjected to the statutory and disciplinary regime of his previous position, but entirely subjected to the status of his new work"[1]

Let us review these positions.

II.3.1- active service

There are two forms of active service[2].

a. Active service per se

A civil servant, who effectively carries out the duties he was appointed for, or works in an equivalent employment in any other State administration is said to be in active service.

b. Active service by assimilation : leaves and further training courses

According to article 51 of the 1994 general rules and regulations the following situations are assimilated to active service : casual or special leave, annual, sick or maternity leave, military service, training or further training, and release from duty for trade union activities.

These positions of active service by assimilation are governed by particular rules :

b.1- Administrative leave

Decree n° 2000/689/PM of september 13, 2000 rules the regime of administrative leaves. They come up after twelve months of effective service, last thirty (30) consecutive days totally paid, including all the benefits the worker is entitled to. The leave is granted by decision of the Head of the ministerial Department concerned, for civil servants of central services, and by decision of the Governor or the senior divisional officer for those of external services ;

b.2- Sick leave is granted to a civil servant in case of persistent illness duly certified by a Government approved medical officer. It should be an illness that prevents, him from carrying out his duties. The concerned must produce a file including a stamped application at the current rate

---

[1] Refer to AUBY (J.M. et DUCOS ADER (R.), *Droit Administratif : Fonction Publique-Biens publics-Travaux publics-Expropriation-Urbanisme-Construction.*
Refer to the Law of april 3, 1955, ordinance of 1959 and a decree of december 30, 1959.

[2] See the general rules and regulations of the Public Service of the State. Decree n° 94/199 of october 7, 1994, article 51.

and a medical certificate delivered by his usual doctor. The sick leave can be possibly extended, up to *ninety (90) days* by decision of the Head of the ministerial department concerned and more than ninety (90) days by the Minister in charge of the public service after approval of the competent health board.

Cumulated and adjourned administrative annual leaves are forbidden.

The schedule of annual leave is drawn up by the minister concerned, the governor or the senior divisional officer, after consultation with the workers concerned.

A prolonged sick leave is granted the worker who fails to recover after six (6) months.

The total periods should not exceed three (3) years for civil servants with less than fifteen (15) years of service, and five (5) years, for those with over fifteen (15) years of service from 1st January of the year of the illness.

It is now up to the Minister of public service, on production of a medical certificate delivered by the usual doctor, to renew the extended six-month periods of leave. Civil servants, who are on extended sick leave, during the first five years of illness, keep their complete index-based salary to which may be added all family allowances. During the next three (3) years, they are paid half of the indexed salary plus the total social allowances.

The period covering the extended sick leave must absolutely be communicated by any means leaving written traces through the hierarchy to the Minister of Public service, if there is a change of residence.

In case of change of residence, the concerned must keep the minister of public service informed every six (6) months.

Every six (6) months, he must send to the minister of public service a medical report from his usual doctor.

Besides, a civil servant who unduly benefits from a prolonged sick leave incurs his immediate dismissal without prejudice of penal proceedings. The medical doctor in collusion is at once sued before the permanent disciplinary council of the public service if he is a civil servant.

The Minister of public service requests the president of the national medical council to start a disciplinary procedure against him.

When the maximum duration of the extended sick leave expires, the restored civil servant, after approval of the health board, is either reinstated in a job corresponding to his professional qualification, or automatically put on admitted to retirement if he is proved definitively unfit to serve.

His pension is increased with a life annuity according to the regulations applicable to civil pensions.

b.3- Maternity leave

Maternity leave is granted by decision of the head of the ministerial department concerned for female civil servants of central services, and by decision of the governor or the divisional officer for those of external services. A copy of the decision is sent to the minister of public service who by order further determines the authorities competent to grant the leave.

The maternity leave covers a period of four weeks before the expected date of childbirth and ten weeks from childbirth.

It can be prolonged for six (06) weeks in case of duly stated, illness related to the pregnancy or childbirth.

It can be extended for four (04) weeks for the civil servant who gives birth while still in active services, to cover the complete period of fourteen (14) weeks.

It is requested by a female civil servant through the presentation of the certificate of her six-month pregnancy.

She is entitled to her entire salary.

After resuming duty, the mother has a (one-hour) rest per day to breast feed her child until he is fifteen months.

b.4- Leave of absence or authorizations

Special authorizations and leaves of absence are granted on duly justified written requests.

The special authorizations are issued by the heads of the user ministerial departments in the central services, the regional Governors at the level of regions, the senior divisional officers for divisions and the divisional officers for districts.

Some special authorizations which are not taken into account in the calculation of annual leaves, can be granted to civil servants for family events or to fulfil a mission of public interest :

- three (03) working days for the childbirth of a legitimate spouse ;
- five (05) days in the event of, marriage or death of the spouse.

These special authorizations are prescribed within ten (10) days of the occurrence of the event.

Leave of absence can be exceptionally given for duly justified personal reasons.

Any new leave of absence beyond ten days cumulation during the same year is deducted from the next annual administrative vacation. Special authorizations concern family events (birth, marriage, death) and leave of absence apply to the other cases.

b.5- Military service

A civil servant can assume duty in the military service for two reasons : either undergoing military training or participation in actions of national defence.

The civil servant called up for military service maintains his salary. He is subject to the military laws and regulations.

A certificate evaluating his behaviour is delivered to him by the military authority at the end of his military service.

This certificate is taken into account in the evaluation report in view of his promotion. It serves as an assessment for the worker.

b.6- Training or further training

Civil servants undergoing training or further training are considered to be in active service.

He must get a prior authorization to attend a seminar, a training course or a further training course[1]. Failure to do so, may exposed him to

[1] Refer to decree n° 2000/679/PM of september13, 2000 organizing the permanent training of civil servants, in particular articles 5 and 6.

disciplinary sanctions and the may be considered irregularly absent as having deserted his duty post.

A civil servant who wishes to undertake studies or personal researches during working time must request a leave of absence or, eventually, his retirement by anticipation.

Here the obligation to fully assume his duties is prevailing.

An interesting question arises. Will he be readmitted into a public service ? In our opinion, a leave of absence would be more advisable.

The Administration can also, due to operational requirements, select a civil servant on duty to pursue specialized training or further training, or carry out special studies with a view to increasing his efficiency and performance.

II.3.2- Secondment

Secondment was defined by article 110 in the former general rules and regulations : as *"the position of a civil servant assigned away from his original corps, but who in his new structure continues to benefit, from the advancement and retirement rights of the corps of origin"*.

The current 1994 general rules and regulations retained the same elements but in two phases :

- First in article 70 : "*Secondment shall be the position of a civil servant who is temporarily assigned away from his duty post* " ;

- Then in article 78 (2nd paragraph) : "*A civil servant on secondment shall continue to enjoy his advancement and pension rights*".

We remark that this situation is still different from the "secondment" of the French public service where civil servants are entirely subjected to the rules of the new corps.

A civil servant on secondment is put outside his corps. However, he continues to benefit from the **rights to advancement and retirement pension from this corps**.

He is temporarily outside his place of duty to serve in :

- a State institution provided for by the Constitution, by law or regulations ;

- Local governments or companies, state corporations or para-statal ;

- State-owned companies ;

- Private structures involved in activities of general interest or associations assuring missions of general interest.

He can be assigned to work in international or non-governmental organizations.

Cameroonian law also recognizes the case of automatic secondment to perform the duties of member of government, public elective functions or mandate as trade-unionist.

We can distinguish the different types by successively considering two factors : the willingness of the civil servant and the role of the body where he is on secondment.

a. Role of the civil servant as criterion of qualification for the secondment

Three (03) positions can be considered.

a-1- Secondment on request of the civil servant

The wish of the concerned is essential ; he asks to be seconded in his own interest. He can obtain it if the body to which he wants to be seconded and the Minister under whom he works have given their approval.

a.2- Automatic secondment

Here the civil servant plays no role, the supervising minister of the body where he is to work in secondment makes a proposal after approval by the user minister. This procedure seems to concern civil servants of the general administration corps. As the minister in charge is the decision-maker, it is a way of adapting to decentralization as regards the management of staff (2nd paragraph article 7 of decree n° 94/199 of october 7th, 1994).

In the past, the condition of essential validity of such a procedure depended on the advantages attached to the new employment, which had to be at least equivalent to those paid in the administration of origin. A more favourable status is therefore the soothing balm for an automatic secondment.

a.3- Secondment by right

Secondment by right is established by order of the minister in charge of the public service for civil servants called to carry out duties as member of government, sit in parliament as parliamentarian or senator, or exercise a full time elective mandate as a representative elected by universal suffrage or as a trade-unionist. Here, the secondment lasts only for as long as the duration of the mandate or duties.

In principle, "*a civil servant on probation*" or in the course of integration can be put on secondment to take up elective duties or as member of government.

b. Secondment institution as a distinction criterion

Secondments can take place in several organizations :

- State institutions provided for by the Constitution, the law or regulations. A wide variety of structures fall within range (the Parliament, the Presidency, state and para-statal companies...) ;

- *Local authorities* or public corporations or para-statals ;

- National private enterprises ;

- Private bodies involved in activities of general interest, or associations providing services of general interest ;

-International or non-governmental organizations.

Really, a civil servant can be henceforth put on secondment anywhere, be it in the public or private sector, in either internal or international bodies.

c. Duration of the secondment

Secondment comes into effect, depending on the case, from the date the act of secondment is signed, the act of appointment to the government published, or publication of final results of the election.

A copy of the act is sent to the minister of finance by the competent authorities and to the minister of public service for the civil servant seconded by right (minister, senator or deputy).

What is the duration of secondment ?

The answers differ according to the cases :

- The civil servant on secondment by right ends his secondment with the termination of his mandate of deputy, senator or the end of his mission as a trade-unionist or member of Government ;

- We can also argue that in a reverse way, the automatic secondment can be revoked by the same authority who ordered it, or on demand of the organization where the civil servant was sent.

"Secondment shall essentially be voidable" (article 75 paragraph 1 of the 1994 general rules and regulations of the public service).

It may be terminated at any moment by order of the very minister who signed the act. Also it can be terminated on request of the administration of origin of the concerned or the structure receiving him, provided that the demand is made at least three months before the date proposed for the termination.

The retirement of a civil servant who has reached the age limit also ends the secondment.

Is there still another case of secondment termination ?

A part from the cases of secondment, the civil servant cannot be seconded in the following circumstances :

-If he does not show proof of a minimum **of five (5) years of work experience** ;

-If he is under to disciplinary proceedings or has not been yet rehabilitated following disciplinary measures.

Experience and expertise are thus prerequisite to secondment, in the interest of the organizations concerned.

The above condition seems to block the way for young civil servants having a stay-at-home attitude in the administrations and who yearn to join lucrative organizations because of the meagre salaries of the Public service.

If one of these conditions is not met, can the secondment be interrupted with the civil servant losing the new benefits acquired in the organization of secondment ?

The law renders secondment an "essentially precarious revocable position ". Does that mean discretionary ?

The general labour law could have mentioned the severance pay or amicable separation allowance.

When the secondment expires, the civil servant is necessarily reinstated in his administration of origin, in a position corresponding to his professional qualification.

He may be reinstated in excess number, to fill the soonest vacancy. The new job has to equal the *grade and qualifications* of the concerned person.

After spending ten consecutive years in secondment, a civil servant who meets the conditions stipulated by the statutory provisions governing access to jobs or jobs of the service where he is seconded, can request through written application and after approval of the Minister concerned to definitively work in the organization.

Six (06) months before reaching retirement age, the aforementioned can demand his final integration by right at his current position or postulate for another employment ; that allows him to defer the retirement date.

A State employee who, at the expiration of the secondment, does not resume the job made available for him by the Administration within one month, is liable to be automatically dismissed. It simply has to correspond to his profile and grade.

Can he dispute it and make it a contentious matter ? *A priori*, yes, if the position does not match the profile.

d. Effects of secondment on status

Secondment is sought because it affects the status of the civil servant and the salary on secondment.

d.1 The effects on the status of the civil servant :

The seconded civil servant is temporarily placed outside his usual work base. He is for a while put at the disposal of his administration or another body which is going to use his services, and dispose of him.

He is in a legal and statutory situation. He is still entitled to benefit from advancement and pension rights.

He remains subjected to the rules of the General Rules and Regulations particularly on disciplinary matters. Besides, he continues to advance in his original cadre.

However, he remains subjected to all the rules and regulations in force of the body of secondment, notwithstanding exceptions provided under by the current laws and regulations, general legal principles and case law.

He is subjected to a new hierarchical subordination in carrying out his duties. The new immediate hierarchy is in charge of his evaluation. The latter may inflict him sanctions lighter than demotion and dismissal.

Other sanctions may be inflicted only according to the rules of his corps and the procedure of common law by duly authorized authorities.

d.2- Effects on wages

The seconded civil servant is paid by the body of secondment.

His salary must be at least equivalent to his indexed salary in the public service. It should not be lower than the global remuneration paid to the staff of the body of secondment carrying out similar duties. Seniority allowances are taken into account if necessary. Secondment generally conveys promises of a better salary status ; that is why it is so appreciated and sought after by civil servants.

A civil servant on secondment who still receives salary from the Public service is at once sued before the Permanent Disciplinary Council of the Public Service and faces legal proceedings for embezzlement. The amounts duly paid must be returned. No service, no salary !

The seconded civil servant remains affiliated to his pension scheme, except if he is on secondment to an international organisation or carries out elective duties.

In case he acquires some pension rights or allowances from the body of secondment, his retirement pension rights or other allowances paid by the State are suspended.

He sustains, in view of the constitution of his retirement pension from the State, statutory deductions calculated on the basis of his indexed salary of the Public service.

Deductions operated for the retirement pension are paid monthly by the body of secondment to the Treasury. The organization reserves for the Treasury his statutory contribution as an employer.

The body of secondment has to show Proof of payments of deductions and of the employers' contribution for pension. The seconded civil servant is in no way accountable for failures of the organization employing him. His pension should not be affected.

The problem of transfer traceability to the treasury is recurrent.

III.3.3- Temporary release

Article 81 of the 1994 general rules and regulations of the public service accurately defines this situation :

"Temporary release shall be the position of a civil servant who is temporarily authorized to close performing his duties of the cadre to which he belongs, and for the duration of this period ceases to enjoy his rights in respect of emoluments, advancement and pension ".

Like secondment, it is a period spent outside the usual structure.

But the difference lies in the fact that he loses his right to advancement, pension and also to payment.

The order granting the leave is signed by the minister in charge of the administration of origin of the civil servant. The minister of public service and, if necessary, the user minister are informed of the act.

For civil servants belonging to the general administration corps, the release is granted by an order of the minister of public service, after approval of the user Minister.

Temporary leave of absence may be used to undertake economic and financial activities, opening the door to the private sector.

a. Release modalities

There has been a remarkable development in the statutory texts :

- release (article 128 of the former general rules and regulations) does not exist any more in the present texts. In the past it was decided by the President of the Republic for a maximal duration of five (05) years, the concerned's family allowances were maintained. He had to have held high-level political or administrative positions in state or para-statal corporations or international organisations ; the measure might occur at the termination of service ;

- ex officio release was granted at the end of a long-term sick leave when the civil servant was susceptible to be cured. It was granted for a renewable period of one (01) year. It is no more mentioned.

Today (1994 general rules and regulations) release on request appears to be the main mode.

It is granted on request of the civil servant for the following reasons :

- self convenience for a duration not exceeding two (02) years ;

- to undertake artistic, cultural, social, economic and financial activities for a duration of three (03) years renewable tacitly ;

- to undertake studies or research during the period.

On request the spouse of a member of government or other important personality and a civil servant can be put or released on secondment if their partner has been appointed in a cameroonian diplomatic or consular mission abroad, an international, or non-governmental organization abroad or within the country, in a locality where the duties do not match his specialization.

Release can also be granted to a civil servant whose dependent child is in a state of health necessitating his constant presence, or whose spouse has been sent on training abroad.

We must emphasize that the general rules and regulations of 1994 took foremost into account the different status of the spouse, government member or other high personality, civil servant appointed to a cameroonian diplomatic or consular mission, international or non governmental body abroad, or admitted into a training course abroad.

This implies an overall effort to move spouses closer and preserve the family unit.

Besides, it was decided and maintained that the spouse on release, exceptionally, continues to benefit from advancement rights on the basis of the last evaluation, but without financial impact. He must have paid his statutory contributions to have the rights to pension.

They have the franchise during elections of staff representatives within the organs of management.

In that case the duration of the release is not deductible from longevity advantages giving right to a pension.

We should bear in mind that release cannot be granted to civil servants who have been suspended or subject to legal proceedings. It should not be a refuge for disciplinary delinquents.

b. Legal regime release : duration and end

There are three (03) modes of terminating release :

- by an act of the administration ;

- on request of the civil servant concerned after having duly given six months (06) prior notice to the competent minister ;

- at the time of the statutory age-limit for retirement, since it should not be a refuge for a civil servant having attained the age limit and susceptible to go on retirement.

What about the one who refuses to return to his administration of origin at the term of release ? In the provisions of the former general rules and regulations, it led to automatic dismissal.

It was generally admitted that the minister of public service, the then sole authority competent to grant release, could at any time proceed to appropriate inquiries to make sure that the activity of the civil servant on granted matched the request, and terminate it if the results are not satisfactory. The concerned was consequently reinstated in his corps of origin.

It would seem normal that such a power has been attributed and extended to other ministers of the civil servants administration of origin. The public ban on forging documents essentially pleads in this direction.

II.4- EVALUATION AND ADVANCEMENT

Civil servants were, like in the french system imported to Cameroon, traditionally assessed through a grading system with mark allocation from 0 to 20[1].The mark was bearing the general comment of the immediate superior.

Grading was the main support for advancement, since advancement was conditioned by good grades.

---

[1] Refer to AUBY (J. M.) and DUCOS ADER (R.), *Droit Administratif 1ère Partie : la Fonction publique,* Dalloz, pp. 105-107.

The notion of evaluation of professional performances replaced the standard procedure of grading[1].

This is really a major innovation to be gradually put into force.

II.4.1- Generalities on the assessment of professional performances

Assessment replaced grading with appropriate modes of application, and specific consequences.

a. Institution of the evaluation system

"*At the end of the financial year and no later than 31 August of each year, the professional performance of each civil servant shall be assessed in terms of the* ***objectives*** *assigned to him, their achievement* ***deadline*** *and the* ***results*** *obtained*", as provided for in article 42 of the 1994 General Rules and Regulations.

A special text, decree n°2001/108/PM of 20th march 2001, defines the statutory modes of professional evaluation.

It should be noted that the financial year has been coupled with the calendar year. February 28th should thus replace august 31st.

This system applies to all civil servants in office, as well as trainees in a probationary period in a job of the administration, two (02) months before the end of the training course.

It applies "mutatis mutandis" to the public agents under the Labour code mindful of the reservation of specific or special texts.

Civil servants on secondment are evaluated following the current rules in the body of secondment.

The evaluation system is a remarkable innovation. Formally decreed it has replaced “in principle" the grading system.

The immediate competent hierarchy must objectively evaluate the staff placed under his authority.

Abstaining from doing it or not doing it properly **constitutes a disciplinary offence**[1]. This provision is drawn from the former general

[1] Refer to decree n° 2001/108/PM of march 20, 2001 fixing the modes of assessment of professional skills of civil servants, in TEKAM Jean, above mentioned work, pp. 248-264.

rules and regulations ; it is the only example of disciplinary offence predetermined by texts.

The 1994 general rules and regulations further stipulates : "*evaluation in regularization is not authorized except in case of absolute necessity duly documented by the immediate superior*" (decree n°2001/108/ PM of march 20th, 2001, paragraph 3).

In our humble opinion, this provision seems very difficult to apply since in practice, grading by regularization has become a rule and even the only possible way because of the various dysfunctions prevailing in our administration (frequent report losses ; need to reconstitute files and careers of the seconded civil servants).

b. Appropriate modes of evaluation

Which are the evaluation criteria and process ?

The fundamental evaluation criterion is results obtained vis-à-vis of the objectives defined by the immediate superior according to norms established by all administrations.

The following elements are taken into account in any evaluation : identification and profile of the job holder, detailed description of the job as defined by the organization chart or the immediate superior, exhaustive enumeration of the tasks entrusted, objectives set by the immediate superior after interview, description of the material, human and financial means used to execute work, action plan elaborated by the state employee to reach the objectives set by the immediate superior. Funds must be made available to implement objectives.

What is evaluated ?

The qualities requested vary with the ranks of the civil servants and the types of tasks executed.

Personal character and professional skills are most required qualities, particularly : managerial skill, public-service awareness, organizational and work method, duty conscientiousness, **work carefully and quickly done**, punctuality, assiduousness, flexible relations with the public and good relations with the hierarchy.

---

[1] Article 43 of the general rules and regulations of the public service, paragraphs 1 and 2 (decree 94/199).

The evaluation form is divided into two parts : the first part indicates the assessment criteria and qualities required for the considered work, and the second part concerns the evaluation.

The first part is signed by the immediate superior, and failure to do so may in cur disciplinary sanctions. The new financial year today places this period at the end of february.

The concerned civil servant countersigns the form with the mention "read and approved".

The immediate superior must put a mark in figures matching the appraisal and assessment of performance results :

- Above 18/20, excellent ;
- Between 18/20 and 17/20 ; very good ;
- Between 16/20, 15/20 and 14/20, good ;
- Between 13/20 and 12/20, averagely good ;
- Between 11/20 and 10/20, average ;
- Lower than 10/20, bad.

The mark must be based on the selected criteria. He must indicate and describe the results to eventually facilitate the work of the administrative judge if a dispute arises.

How does the chain of evaluation work ?

c. The evaluation chain

It is **a highly hierarchical system** where the process is performed at two levels : by the immediate superior at the first level and the senior officer above him, at the second level.

The immediate superior fills and signs the evaluation form in four copies and transmits it to the senior officer at the second level.

The latter may validate or invalidate the general appraisal and marks.

In case of invalidation, he must give his motives.

Finally the average of the two (2) marks attributed determines the assessment ; it may include a decimal place.

The immediate superior who does the appreciation plays an essential role in terminating it.

The command chain starts from the chief of service to the sub-director, the director to the general secretary and lastly to the minister or the head of diplomatic mission. The regional governor too intervenes at a significant stage.

The authority in charge of the final evaluation assigns the various copies of the form.

The original copy is sent to the minister of public service. The second form is sent to the ministerial department head to whom the assessed agent reports. The third copy is returned to the immediate superior destined for the evaluated agent. The fourth copy is intended for the regional delegation of the public service for public agents working in external services or to the minister of public service for those working in the central services.

c.1- Assessment of civil servants of central services

At the first level, the head of bureau and the chief of service at the second level appraise the civil servants who do not hold any position of responsibility ; the deputy planning officer studies and the planning officer play the same role in survey bodies and firms.

At the first level the chief of service and the sub-director at the second level both evaluate heads of bureau.

Sub-directors and those in the same category are evaluated at the first level by directors and at the second level by the competent secretary general.

The secretary general and the minister are competent for directors and those in the same category.

The minister, at the last level, evaluates the Secretary general of his ministry.

c.2- Civil servants of external services

The evaluation cycle works in a different way as regards the civil servants of external services.

The minister in charge of territorial administration alone evaluates the governors.

The governor at the first level and the minister at the final level evaluate the senior divisional officers (SDO) and the Secretaries general of regions.

As concerns divisional officers (DO), the assessment is performed by the senior Divisional officer at the first level, and next by the governor of the region.

The SDO and the DO are both respectively competent at the first and second level to assess sub divisional deputies.

As concerns heads of the governor's services, the evaluation is done at the first level by the immediate superior, then the first deputy DO and at the second level by the senior divisional officer.

For general staff working in the services of administrative authorities, the evaluation is made at the first level by the immediate superior and at the second level by the senior officer above him.

c.3- Civil servants in technical structures

The evaluation of the civil servants in technical structures is done in the following way :

- regional delegates or workers of similar status are appraised by the secretary general of the region at the first level and then by the governor at the second level ;

- divisional delegates and those of the same status are evaluated at the first level by the First deputy SDO and at the second level by the senior divisional officer ;

- for the sub divisional delegates and those of the same status, the evaluation is done at the first level by the deputy of the divisional officer and at the second level by the divisional officer ;

- the divisional delegate at the first level and the regional delegate at the last level assess executives of the divisional delegations ;

- the immediate superiors, at the first and second level estimate respectively the execution of the regional, divisional and district services.

c.4- Civil servants on duty in diplomatic missions

The assessment of civil servants on duty in diplomatic missions is as follows :

- heads of diplomatic representations are assessed by the ministry of external relations at the first and last level ;

- by the ambassador or the chargé d'affaires, for the immediate assistants of the ambassador or the chargés d'affaires.

- for the support staff, the evaluation is done at the first level by the head of the representation supervising the service concerned, at the second level by the ambassador or the chargé d'affaires.

c.5- Other cases of evaluation

There are special modalities guiding the evaluation of civil servants in extended leave or in detention sanctioned by a decision of acquittal or release. His marks for the year (s) of absence are equal to the average marks of the last two years of effective service.

Civil servants on secondment who carry out duties as government members or have an elective mandate are advanced without evaluation.

To conclude, what can we finally think about this system ?

Does it entail security for the civil servant ?

What is the nature of the act stemming from the process of evaluation ?

d. Nature of the act stemming from the process of evaluation ?

The traditional case law of the French administrative jurisdiction had considered grading at first as a mere preparatory act for later administrative decisions (CE 2nd May to october, 1937, Morel R. 833). Then the Council of State accepted them as administrative acts (on CE November 23rd, 1963, Camara R.627 AJ 1962 II.687). Marks were no mere acts of internal order but administrative acts.

Mr. Tekam Jean mentions the evaluation systems currently in application in other african countries.

In Burkina Faso, the classical grading system remains in force. The worker is authorized to use their rights or make remarks during the procedure before being attributed the final mark.

In Zaire, the grading was replaced by a "quotation" based on merit, ranging from "mediocre" to "excellent".

In Congo, the minister of public service designates every year 10 % of the best workers and 10 % with the poorest performances.

We must notice that in Cameroon the system of evaluation by objectives is yet to be effectively put in place. What are the reasons ?

This kind of evaluation form seems not yet to be operational. That is why, as the only option classical grading continues to be applied...[1]

Our opinion would be that the evaluation process in Cameroon is an administrative procedure generating administrative acts susceptible to be subjected to the litigious control of power abus.

All it takes is to have *the quality and the interest to act*[2].

II.4.2- Consequences of the evaluation : impact on the career

The assessment of the civil servant or State employee has consequences and tangible effects on his career. Whether the grading is excellent, acceptable or mediocre, it certainly has an impact on the evolution of his career.

a. Excellent service and reward

Article 18 of decree n° 2001/108/PM of march 20th, 2001 stipulates that a civil servant who is considered having an excellent output can receive from the State one of the rewards enumerated in the general rules and regulations of the public service.

The 1994 general rules and regulations of the public service offer rewards to a civil servant who has been outstanding in service particularly through "*his dedication to the public interest*" and "*special contribution to increasing the output and efficiency of the service*" (article 111).

These rewards are :

- letter of encouragement ;

---

[1] See TEKAM, *Op cit.* p. 256.

[2] Refer to the outlook of the Cameroonian administrative judge on the matter :

CFJ/CAY order n° 178 of march 29, 1972 E. MOUELLE KOULA versus Federal Republic of Cameroon RCD n° 3, p. 54.

CFJ/CAY order n° 178 of march 28, 1967, AMOUGOU Philippe and Mrs NKOA Martine versus the State of Cameroon.

CFJ/CAY order n° 188 of march 28, 1972, WAMBO Télesphore versus Federate State of Eastern Cameroon RCD n°3.

- letter of congratulations ;
- official testimonial of satisfaction ;
- distinction of merit ;
- certificate of Excellence ;
- honorary membership.

Other rewards can, when necessary, be created and organized, by special texts.

The rewards are awarded by public authorities :

- the user minister, the senior divisional officer or the governor sends a letter of support and a letter of congratulations on proposal of the immediate superior ;

- the minister of public service on proposal motivated by the immediate superior approved by the user minister, awards the official testimony of satisfaction and the merit distinction, making sure he does this after approval by the joint administrative board ;

- The Prime minister, head of government awards the **diploma of excellence** on proposal of the minister of public service supported by an elaborate report, after **approval of the joint administrative board**. The minister of public service hands it over solemnly to the laureate ;

- Lastly, **the honorary diploma is conferred by decree of the president of the Republic**, on proposal of the Prime minister supported by an elaborate report and after approval of the joint administrative board. The status of the laureate is then determined by decree of the Prime minister. He authorizes the civil servant on retirement to carry the title corresponding to the highest position attained during his career. At the same time he can be granted an allowance as determined in the list of civil pensions. He must have obtained at least a distinction of **merit** or a **certificate of excellence** during his career. The applicant for the honorary membership must make a written request. He must have never been inflicted any disciplinary sanction or sewed a penal sentence. Honorary membership is conferred by the president of the Republic. This distinction can be lost together with the attendant benefits in the event of condemnation to a custodial prison sentence.

The instrument granting the reward shall be notified to the beneficiary, with a record kept in his personal file and, when necessary, rendered public by the administration.

What are the effects of awards ?

a.1- The effects of awards

Rewards entitle its recipient to advancement and upgrading.

Hence, the official testimonial of satisfaction entitles to an additional grade level whenever the same civil servant receives such award twice (2 times) within 3 (three) consecutive years.

The merit entitles to one grade level ; whereas the certificate of excellence gives right to two (02) grade levels. The notification for upgrading is signed by the minister of public service. It comes into effect from the date of signature, except if the interested party has already attained the ceiling.

These bonuses have a pecuniary impact on wages.

What is the legal basis of awards ?

a.2- The legal basis of awards

Are they administrative acts or government acts unlikely to be subjected to controls of the administrative judge ? Can a civil servant bring legal action in dispute or for abuse of power ?

In our opinion, all seems to indicate the administrative nature of these acts that are liable to contentious recourse, since :

- the formal form is an order or a decree ;

- it is signed by high officials such as the head of State, the Prime minister, and the minister in charge of the public service ;

- these authorities are entrusted with the duty of evaluation-notation, an administrative attribute having as object an administrative act.

The 1994 general rules and regulations renewed guarantees of impartiality through the implication of the joint administrative board and the head of State to grant the honorary certificate.

It is worth mentioning that this time, only the improvement of incremental position is involved. Upgrading in class and rank are no longer provided for (article 191 of the rules of 1972). The civil servant must have a legal status and an interest in acting (CFJ / CA decree n° 178 of march 28th, 1972 Wambo Télesphore versus the Federated State of Eastern Cameroon RCD n° 3).

b. Acceptable output and letter of observation

A "*public agent whose output is considered acceptable receives a letter of observation about his way of rendering service*" (article 18 of the decree n° 2001/108/PM of march 20, 2001, paragraph 2).

The average score is equivalent to 11/20 and 10/20. The immediate superior justifies the score and enters it in the evaluation form.

This score could have been accompanied with a warning discussion required because the civil servant or State agent who has a poor performance may improve his performance after this talk.

c. Mediocre performance and summons to appear before a joint commission

"*The civil servant whose output is considered mediocre is summoned before the joint administrative board*" (article 18, paragraph 3 of the decree n° 2001/108/PM of march 20th, 2001).

The question is : what is the purpose of the summons before the Commission ? The aforementioned provision aims at article 119 of the 1994 general rules and regulations, which declares that the "*termination of service of a civil servant may result from" :* professional incompetence observed from the evaluation results, in particular after a delayed incremental promotion at the end of a four (04) years period.

The sanction seems to occur at the end of four (04) years that means two consecutive unsuccessful evaluations.

Professional incompetence is stated by the minister concerned or the Minister of public service. In the previous case, he informs the minister of public service. This one refers to the joint administrative board which declares, if necessary, the dismissal of the civil servants concerned on written notice.

The same procedure applies for physical incapacity as the agent appears before the health council.

The dismissed civil servant receives an allowance three (03) times equivalent to his monthly indexed salary in case of professional incompetence.

We remind that this allowance is twelve (12) times the monthly indexed payment in case of physical disability, and twenty-four (24) times the monthly indexed payment in case of job loss.

These allowances are paid at once at the dismissal.

The act pronouncing the dismissal of a civil servant liquidates all his rights, including his retirement pension.

To conclude, we should remember that evaluation- as well as awards - have a significant impact on the career of a civil servant or public agent.

d. Output, excellence and advancement

(1) "E*valuation conditions the career evolution of a civil servant, particularly as regards his advancement*".

(2) " *The appreciations below, with a matching score, give way to the advancement of a civil servant or the appointment on a permanent basis of a trainee : excellent, very good, good, averagely good* " (article 17 of decree n° 2001/108/PM of march 20th, 2001).

The required score ranges from 18/20 to 12/20. They give right to promotion by merit. They are expressed in whole numbers.

Advancement in incremental position of a civil servant inside a class is conditioned by a favourable evaluation. It occurs every two (2) years.

II.4.3- Advancement

A civil servant's career is not a quiet, straight and uniform one. There are all along beneficial changes. Advancement aims at improving the condition of a civil servant :

- either through upgrading opening the way for him to hold senior duties,

- or through incremental advancement, entitling him to a higher salary.

Career promotions in grades, classes, and ranks within the same cadre are continuous.

We will proceed by studying the types of promotions and the processes giving right to them.

a. Types of promotions

It would appear the 1994 general rules and regulations renewed four (4) types of promotions for civil servants :

a.1- Advancement in incremental position

It occurs within a class. It depends on how favourable the worker has been assessed. It happens every two (02) years. It is materialized by a salary increase, upgrading to the next salary index, however not involving a job transfer, or change in rank.

a.2- Advancement in class.

It comes within the same rank. It depends both on the evolution and seniority of the civil servant.

The seniority required in that case is two (02) years at, the last level of the civil servant's class.

A favourable assessment is also needed to give access to level or class promotion. The average evaluation mark obtained in two (02) consecutive years must not be less than 12/20.

The same rank can include several classes.

a.3- Rank promotion

Promotions in rank are conditioned by the seniority and favourable evaluation of the civil servant. They may also result from a new professional qualification or a civil service examination successfully passed.

This promotion can come before the term of the deadline of two (02) consecutive years from the date the civil servant attained the last level of the second class within his rank. He must not be less than forty (40) years of age.

The advancement in rank after a new professional qualification starts from the date of obtaining the corresponding certificate for the civil servant in service, and from the date of resumption of duty, at the term of release.

Advancement in rank gives the opportunity to hold higher positions.

a.4- Promotion to senior officer

The passage from officer to senior officer takes place through a competitive examination.

Professional competitive examinations thus enable civil servants to move up, not only within a rank but to step up to the immediate upper officer grade (article 13 of decree n° 2000/696 of september 13th, 2000 laying down the general regime of civil service examinations).

b. Promotion methods

The 1994 general rules and regulations of the public service establish several promotions methods : on preliminary evaluation, following a reward, after a successful civil service examination, after a change in professional qualification or acquisition of professional or university certificates.

b.1- Advancement following a competition examination

Civil service examinations are a mode of recruitment of civil servants. Professional competitive examinations are special as they "*ensure promotion in rank within a cadre or movement to a cadre immediately above*"[1].

It is thus a mode of promotion and advancement for enterprising civil servants who wish to improve their status. It is one of the promotion methods within the said cadre. Such advancement is continuous.

The interested civil servant enrols for the professional competitive exam when it is launched. The age-limit is of **forty five** (45) years for access to the jobs of category C, and **fifty** (50) years for categories A and B.

The posts to be filled are opened by competitive examination and specified by the terms of the special rules and regulations.

The professional competitive examination channel is not exclusive : it opens the door to advancement by seniority.

b.2- Advancements following an award

Awards, as earlier emphasized, entitle the civil servant to advancement :

- Incremental position advancement, in case of **official testimonial** of satisfaction awarded twice (2 times) to the same civil servant within three (3) consecutive years ;

- The advancement by one incremental position in case of distinction of **merit**, and two (02) incremental positions for the **certificate of excellence**.

---

[1] Refer to article 13 of decree n° 2000/696/PM of september 13, 2000 ruling the system of administrative competitive examinations.

These bonuses are granted by order of the minister of public service who notifies them. They come into effect from the date of signature.

What about the former texts that simply gave preference to civil servants with an equal merit ? The civil servant holding a letter of congratulation and encouragement had priority over his peers with equal merit and seniority when promotion was discretionary. The passage and the rise in incremental positions are now automatic. They are no more, according to the text, a matter of preference that do not give priority to equal merit and seniority.

b.3- Advancement following capacity building

The new 1994 general rules and regulations **grant a bonus for the building of professional capacities.** Promotion is conditioned by a change of professional qualification or the acquisition of professional or university certificates.

It is worth mentioning that any certificate or qualification entitles to promotion only under conditions set forth by the private or special rules and regulations.

The duration and level of the certificate or training must be taken into consideration.

It is necessary to note that several lists of schools specialized in training civil servants have been drawn up. A procedure for equivalences has been also established. These measures can help facilitate disputes likely to arise from this specific promotion procedure.

b.4- Advancement based on longevity of service and selection

Article 77 of the 1972 general rules and regulations of the public service organized two (02) modes of traditionally different promotions : promotion by selection, depending on the grading, and promotion based on longevity of service depending on the time spent in service.

Current regulations did not totally contradict the state of the law. Two traditional principles are considered in their various capacities :

- favourable evaluation ;

- seniority.

Advancement in level takes place every two (02) years and depends on a favourable evaluation. The average mark obtained must be equal to

12/20. The usual procedure at the end of four (04) years is no more in use. Poorly evaluated civil servants risk being dismissed after the joint administrative board is consulted.

Advancements in class within the same rank are also conditioned by longevity in service and by evaluation.

The required longevity is two (02) years from the last incremental position of the class to which the civil servant belongs. Besides he must have got a good evaluation with an average of at least 12/20.

Advancements in rank is conditioned by a favourable evaluation and seniority, except when a new professional qualification or success in a civil service examination intervenes.

He must have spent two (02) years in the higher level of the second class of his rank and be at least forty (40) years old.

Advancement of rank based on a reinforcement of professional capacities (competition or professional qualification) has been reviewed.

The case of civil servants who advance in rank following specialization or after obtaining a university degree, in accordance with the conditions laid down by the private rules and regulations, has also been examined.

The current text remains silent on whether a civil servant can, during his career benefit from several discretionary rank promotions. The former texts prohibited it. But the logic of continuous further training suggests it is not advisable to ban it.

The general rules and regulations no longer limit these advancements to 10% of recruitments, with the option of accumulating these percentages over several years

Other regulations govern promotion by selection and seniority.

c. Other advancement regulations

i) The civil servant must be **registered in the promotion table** to be granted advancement by selection. It is established every year by order of the minister of public service after approval of the joint administrative board. It is an administrative act.

In the past an additional table could be drawn up if the previous one was exhausted before the end of the year. Available job vacancies did not all have to be filled.

ii) Registration in the promotion table is subordinated to a detailed examination of the professional worth of the civil servant having been evaluated by the immediate seniors ;

iii) Promotions occur by merit, in the order determined by the table. The oldest is selected at equal merit or seniority. An award also allows deciding between the interested parties, in favour of the beneficiary of the award.

II.5. TERMINATION OF DUTY

The termination of duties results in the loss of the status of civil servant. It results from resignation, lay off, dismissal or retirement.

Termination of duties may be fortuitously occasioned by death, or initiated by the Administration in cases of lay off, retirement or dismissal, or initiated by the civil servant himself, as in resignation.

II.5.1- Termination on the initiative of the administration

Several hypotheses can be considered : lay off of the civil servant, compulsory retirement, dismissal, revocation of an irregular appointment.

a. Lay off of the civil servant

"Lay off is a measure that finally dismisses the civil servant from the Public Service for cases that are not prompted by disciplinary measures"[1].

It terminates the duties of a public employee for reasons which are not disciplinary. It occurs before retirement.

There are three (03) known cases :

i) In the event of permanent physical disability which is incompatible with the job position held ;

ii) In the event of professional incompetence attested by his assessment results, especially after no advancement in four (04) years ; he must have been badly evaluated during the four (04) years.

---

[1] Refer to articles 118, 119 and 120 of the general rules and regulations of the public service of 1994.

iii) Following special instruments providing for the reorganization of services resulting in job losses without the possibility of redeploying personnel.

A "*civil servant on probation*" is laid off after approval of the "*ad hoc* committee" in case of unsatisfactory probation. The committee is chaired by the minister in charge of the public service.

The minister of public service establishes the physical disability or the professional incompetence. The user minister can also do that.

He refers to the joint administrative committee or the competent health board, as the case may be. On its certified approval if necessary, he declares the lay off of the civil servant concerned.

Besides the potential pension dues, the laid-off worker receives an allowance equivalent to twelve (12) times his monthly indexed salary in case of physical disability ; three (03) times his monthly indexed salary in case of professional incompetence and twenty four (24) times his monthly indexed salary in case of abolition of job position.

In the past the severance pay was increased with family allowances paid at once on departure. It is still the case today.

The instrument terminating the service of a civil servant shall order the payment of all his dues, including his old-age pension where applicable.

b. Dismissal of the civil servant

"*Dismissal shall entail the permanent exclusion of a civil servant from the Public service on the grounds of an offence* "[1].

Dismissal shall be decided by the authority empowered to make appointments.

It may arise from a disciplinary procedure of the Public service.

Dismissal is automatic in some other cases :

i) Desertion from work for thirty (30) consecutive days after a formal warning has been ignored ;

---

[1] Refer to articles 121 and 122 of the general rules and regulations of the public service of 1994.

ii) Loss of the Cameroonian nationality or a custodial prison sentence for a crime or offence of probity (theft, forgery, influence peddling, swindling, fraud, corruption, embezzlement, breach of trust). The punishment can be accompanied with forfeiture as stipulated by the Penal Code[1].

The offence must have entailed a prison sentence of more than six months.

The 1994 general rules and regulations of the public service did not include as it did earlier, the other causes for dismissal :

- condemnations casting a slur on one's honour ;

- house arrest.

Article 176 of the 1994 general rules and regulations of the public service confirms a case of automatic dismissal : a civil servant who, at the term of his secondment, does not within one (01) month reintegrate the job position reserved for him that matches his professional qualification.

Besides, the civil servant who unduly extends his sick leave incurs automatic dismissal, notwithstanding any legal proceedings.

Can the dismissed civil servant be recruited anew into the public service ?

The answer is likely to be in the affirmative but under several conditions :

- satisfy the general conditions of nationality, age, good morality already prescribed ;

- rehabilitation in case of penal condemnation ;

- applying to reintegrate his former corps.

It must be at least five years[2] after the effective date of his dismissal.

---

[1] See article 30 of the penal Code : forfeitures.
Forfeitures consist in the following :
1°Dismissal and exclusion from all public functions, jobs or office ;
2° Incapacity to be a sworn, an assessor, a sworn expert ;
3° Be forbidden to wear decorations ;
4° Be forbidden to serve in the armed forces ;
5° Be forbidden to conduct a school or teach…
See article 65 (paragraph) of the 1994 general rules and regulations.

The wages of the civil servant must be subject to attachment or voluntary assignment.

What of the case of a dismissed civil servant ?

"When dismissal results from an offence which entailed material and/or financial prejudice to the State, the pension of the civil servant in question shall be continuously distrained within the limits of the distrainable quota" (article 22 of the general rules and regulations).

The amount shall not exceed one third of the pension. This is an exceptional measure as pensions are generally not distrainable. The operation lasts until the extinguishment of the prejudice.

c. Retirement

"Retirement marks the normal end of the active employment of the civil servant and shall entitle him to pension paid by the public treasury or any other pension fund"[1].

It is the common mode of termination of a civil servant's activities. As stipulated in the rules and regulations, it gives way to old-age pension.

Retirement may be **before due date**. A civil servant who has put in a minimum of fifteen (15) years can request his retirement before due date. It does not seem to raise any problem.

The minister of the public service orders the admission to retirement.

The said order shall settle the payment of the pension dues of the retired civil servant.

With the attainment of the age limit, no matter the administrative duties on hand by virtue of an individual or collective act, retirement can be automatic, subject to the provisions of special rules and regulations.

The age-limit for retirement is fifty (50) years for categories **C** and **D**, and, fifty five (55) years for the categories **A** and **B**.

The president of the Republic may waive the provisions of the law by reason of the specificity of certain duties, and consequently extend the periods of activity for the civil servant who has attained the age limit.

The provisions on automatic retirement have proven difficult to apply.

---

[1] See articles 123, 124, 125 and 126 of the 1994 general rules and regulations.

Is retirement automatic or is it automatic after the signing of an administrative act, notwithstanding extension by the President ?

Civil servants holding high official positions have often refused to leave their positions as far as a parallel act was not signed.

Is an act of the minister of the public service coupled with a payment of cessation by the minister of finance absolutely required ?

Not in our opinion. **Reaching the age-limit means losing the status of civil servant, therefore automatically being excluded from the public service and, by way of consequence, from any official duty, notwithstanding express prorogation.**

Hence a parallel act is not necessary. A civil servant reaching the age-limit has to leave his position and start the retirement formalities to benefit the payment of his pension.

Old-age pension is paid by the treasury or any other pension fund under conditions laid down by a decree of the president of the Republic[1].

He is entitled to a pension of seniority or to a proportionate pension.

The seniority pension is served to civil servants who have put in at least 25 (twenty-five) years of effective service on the date of retirement.

The proportionate pension is served to : a civil servant who, having reached the age-limit, cannot claim a seniority pension, one who has a permanent and total disability resulting from carrying out duties or occasioned in the course of duties, one who was dismissed without loss of the pension dues, one who came under forfeiture after twenty (20) years of service, or having completed seventeen (17) years of service and has not less than three (03) dependent children.

Retirement before due date offers three main advantages : an increased number of annuities to five (05) years, a bonus incremental position, and an installation payment.

A civil servant who for whatever reason stops his activity cannot benefit from old-age pension, but is entitled to get at once the total deductions operated on his salary as pension contributions during his career.

---

[1] See decree n° 74/759 of august 26, 1974 organizing the civil pensions system. MINFOPRA, Ministry of the public service and administrative reform – Manual on retirement and payment of rights.

As a reminder, the contribution to pension dues went from six percent (6%) up to ten percent (10%) deductions from the indexed salary.

Retirement liquidates the pension dues.

d. Revocation of irregular appointment

The state at any time has powers to revoke any irregular appointment.

The general rules and regulations of the public service contain in this respect several eloquent provisions :

"Any person recruited as a civil servant through established fraudulent means shall, as soon as such fraud is uncovered, be dismissed from the public service by the authority with powers of appointment" article 18 of the 1994 general rules and regulations states.

Besides, legal and civil proceedings may be brought against him. This provision participates in raising the moral standards in the Public service.

Decree n° 2000/696/PM of 13 september 2000 determining the general regime of civil service examinations, while resuming this statement, adds : "**Notwithstanding any criminal and civil proceedings which may be instituted against him,** *any person recruited as a civil servant during a civil service examination through established fraudulent means shall, as soon as the fraud is uncovered, be dismissed from the public service by the authority with powers of appointment*" (article 58).

Furthermore, in the same text (article 9) a civil servant in a cadre of the Public service, candidate for a direct entrance competitive examination in order to enter another corps, is compelled to obtain the prior authorization of the minister of the public service after approval of the user minister.

Which sanction applies in case of violation of this obligation ?

First, this obligation does not exempt from fulfilling all the other conditions required to pass the competitive examination.

Moreover, the violation of this obligation may at any time authorize the revocation of any admission in the said competitive exam, examination or school.

However, recourse to validation of authorizations to change from one cadre to another through retroactive regularization, in such circumstances, is common practice.

This measure turns out to be appropriate and encouraging for civil servants wishing to improve their status and competent enough to do it.

II.5.2- Termination of duties on the initiative of the civil servant : resignation

Two (02) hypotheses exist for the voluntary termination of activities by a civil servant : admission to retirement on request already studied, and resignation.

"*Resignation shall be done in writing, the civil servant clearly stating his desire to finally leave the public service*".

What do we retain from this definition ?

Resignation is a written act. It is not a mere oral declaration, neither a guess. It leaves a written track. It is a "*writ*".

Resignation is a chosen, unequivocal and unilateral manifestation by a civil servant to definitively leave the corps to which he belongs, into which he was integrated.

It is consequently at the initiative of the civil servant who makes the offer of resignation to the minister of the public service through his hierarchy.

Can the initiative be suggested or imposed on him ?

"The Minister in charge of the public service shall be bound to notify the civil servant concerned of the order accepting his resignation, within a period of three (03) months starting from the date of receipt of the letter of resignation. After this period the resignation shall be considered accepted."

At first, the authority with powers of appointment was the only one authorized to accept it within four (04) months starting from the reception of the letter.

Acceptance of the resignation makes it irrevocable.

Is it possible for the civil servant to retrieve his letter before acceptance ? Or change his mind about resigning ?

Acceptance terminates the operation. This means that the concerned may retrieve the letter before it is accepted.

Can the minister in charge of the public service refuse the resignation ? In our opinion he can do it, although the 1994 provisions do not specify any more unlike those of 1972, that the letter of resignation of the civil servant shall be regularly accepted by the authority with powers of appointment.

Any resignation accepted following the above mentioned procedure shall entail the payment of the entitlements of the resigning civil servant, according to the rules and regulations governing civil pensions.

The resigned civil servant remains liable for acts, professional, non professional or personal offences committed in the performance of or in the course of performing his duties.

He remains bound by the obligation of reserve and professional discretion in respect of all facts, documents and information of which he had knowledge as a civil servant. In case of breach of this provision, he may be prosecuted in accordance with the laws in force.

The civil servant who puts an end to his duties in spite of the opposition of the Administration, before the express or tacit acceptance of his letter of resignation by the minister in charge of the public service, is solely responsible.

In the past, the general rules and regulations stipulated that he was dismissed with abolition of his pension rights without prior consultation of the disciplinary council under prejudice of the payment of damages to the State on account of the desertion of his post.

Considering all the abovementioned, we can deduce that prompted, unaccepted or blank resignations are null and void.

II.5.3- Termination by death

"*The duties of a civil servant shall cease with his death*", article 127 of the 1994 general rules and regulations.

Duties shall cease, and logically, nobody shall inherit (1) them ; this, however, is scarcely understood by the family of the deceased who would wish to have their offspring work in the same administration.

The rightful claimants of the deceased are, upon presentation of a statutory file within a period of three (03) months, granted a death benefit and a reversionary pension by the State.

If the death results from an accident due to service or occurring because of or during duty, the death benefit is increased fivefold. A decree of the Prime minister fixes the conditions of payment.

All costs relating to the funeral expenses, coffin and the mortal remains or all other expenses are taken care of by the government.

The government is responsible for the transportation of the legitimate spouses or spouse and minor children as well as their belongings to the usual place of residence.

These are the last benefits granted to a deceased civil servant.

CHAPTER IV

MATERIAL BENEFITS AND OBLIGATIONS OF THE CIVIL SERVANT

Funeral expenses being taken care of are already an evident material benefit. Being a civil servant provides a lot of material benefits including wages earned while still working, old-age pension, etc. These benefits are compensated for by duties, although he also has rights.

I. MATERIAL BENEFITS

Article 27 of the general rules and regulations of the public service stipulates : *"A civil servant shall, in respect of services rendered, be entitled to wages comprising a basic salary corresponding to his index, compulsory family allowances and, where applicable, various allowances and benefits."*

It further underlines : "the conditions for the payment of wages in respect of services rendered shall be determined by decree of the president of the Republic".

I.1- RIGHT TO REMUNERATION

General principles in force shall be examined and elements enumerated.

I.1.1- General principles of remuneration

The civil servant is entitled to remuneration. It is a claim protected by law, an obligation. The remuneration is based on the civil servant's rank paid after service rendered.

a. Legal nature of the remuneration : an obligation and a claim

According to article 27 of the general rules and regulations, a civil servant is "entitled to remuneration". It is a legal obligation for the state, a statutory provision and benefit. It is a fundamental guarantee granted the civil servant by the statutes.

May he relinquish his remuneration and work in return for a symbolic payment ? In our opinion it is a right, it is his right.

However, the statutory nature instituting this right limits its effect. In fact, it is established by decree ; but can a law restrain the right ?

Remuneration is due as soon as a civil servant takes up office, from appointment to installation.

He may in certain cases lose his remuneration, like when he is on release or in military service.

Can he be granted other wages ?

It would sound reasonable that he should be granted allowances, not only wages. For instance, in France, registrars of mortgages collect a tax from people who use their services (the salary of registrars). Tax (direct tax and land tax) collectors participate in the production of fines. Pilots on duty do collect taxes from users.

A salaried worker, unlike a civil servant, has a vested right to his salary by dint of his work contract. The cameroonian civil servant, whose remuneration is laid down by rules and regulations, does not have the same right. It is consequently hard to consider the salary as the price for work, instead of considering the remuneration after a service rendered (as rather a desire to maintain the rank of the civil servant.

Rules and regulations in force protect the remuneration of the civil servant. He may have compulsory deductions from his remuneration, namely taxes, allied taxes, and pension contributions. However, no other deduction may be made from the wages of a civil servant except by attachment or voluntary assignment.

The distrainable or assignable amount cannot exceed one-third of the wages of the civil servant concerned.

The pension contribution amounts to 10% deduction from the indexed salary of the civil servant.

b. Remuneration "after service rendered"

The principle of remuneration after service rendered means that the remuneration cannot be received unless the civil servant has performed his work.

Due payment is done after service is rendered. This statutory principle involves requirement of proof that the service has actually been performed : the right to payment takes effect only as from the installation in his duties.

The administration must always establish a **certificate of assumption of duty.** It may in some cases, even establish a "**certificate of effective presence at work**".

The default of service rendered entails no remuneration.

The loss may be total or partial. Absence from work for any fraction of the day is sanctioned by a deduction whose amount is equal to the corresponding fraction of the indivisible indexed salary.

Service shall be considered as not rendered if :

i) the civil servant fails to work all or part of the working day ;

ii) the civil servant fails to carry out all or part of the duties relating to his job position during the working day.

The abovementioned provisions mostly apply to those who receive a monthly remuneration including deductions.

The administration will rightly refuse to pay the imprisoned civil servant.

The suspended civil servant loses his basic payment right. He preserves, if need be, his family allowances.

I.1.2- Elements of remuneration

The 1994 general rules and regulations under article 27 provide : « *A civil servant shall be entitled to remuneration comprising a basic salary corresponding to his index, compulsory family allowances and, where applicable, various allowances and benefits* ».

Remuneration would therefore comprise :

1. a salary calculated according to the rank, class and incremental position of the civil servant, consequently, according to his classification index, which gives a constant amount called basic salary ;

2. allowances which constitute an addition to the basic salary calculated according to his rank within a corps or the job position held ; these allowances may be : technical bonus, responsibility, car maintenance, housing allowances paid to the civil servant pursuant to special instruments ;

3. miscellaneous bonuses : for civil servants of the higher education corps ;

4. Family allowances, still according to the general rules and regulations.

Does the designation family allowances also cover other benefits ? It is not precisely defined. It should be nevertheless reminded that family allowances have a special and secured system. Their payment is often guaranteed even in the event of sanctions or disciplinary procedure.

I.2- TRAVELLING EXPENSES

The travelling expenses of civil servants and the conditions of the State budgetary provisions for their payment have fostered the production of a special instrument.

Members of government are governed by a different system, as well as armed forces personnel and medical evacuees.

There are various distinctions :

- travelling abroad or within the country ;

- temporary or final transfer of the public servant ;

- status of the public worker and his accompanying group, is it a diplomatic mission where he has been sent to, or a simple tour.

I.2.1- Taking the status of the civil servant into consideration

When travelling expenses are taken care of by the State budget, account is taken of the status of the public worker. This consists in his duties, index, rank and category. Civil servants are divided into IV groups :

- **Group I** is made up of civil servants whose index is equal to or above 870, who may hold such positions as : technical advisers, directors, official representatives, attachés at the presidency or the Prime minister's office, governors and regional secretaries general, secretaries general, presidents and prosecutors of the supreme court, ambassadors, consuls general, consuls and officials of the same status. It also includes all contract workers of the 12th category.

- **Group II** comprises : directors of cabinets, regional heads of division, assistant divisional officers, deputy directors, sub-directors, attachés at the social and economic council, embassy advisors, aid workers, civil servants whose index is at least equal to 590 and under 870, and categories 9 and 10 workers ;

- **Group III** comprises assistant heads of departments, deputy of central services, third secretaries and attachés, civil servants whose index is between 196 and 530, categories 8 and 9 workers ;

- Lastly, **group IV** concerns public workers not holding job positions of responsibility, civil servants whose index is below 196, and workers of category 7 and below.

This special instrument also provides for the civil servant on duty in a consular diplomatic mission, as well as a public worker on training abroad.

Account is also taken of the family unit.

The family of the public worker, that is, the spouse and dependent children, is authorized to travel at the expenses of the administration in the same class as the civil servant concerned.

Children travelling by air with their parents cannot join their parents in first class unless they are under two (02) years of age. Children not accompanied by their parents travel in economy class.

The status of the civil servant is considered in the travel conditions :

- railway transportation class varies according to the classification group of the civil servant ;

- workers of groups I and II are entitled to travel by air even within the national territory ;

- heads of consular and diplomatic missions, technical advisers, civil servants of group I, travel in first class and the president of the Republic may waive this rule for any public worker on special duties ;

- heads of diplomatic and consular missions are entitled to the additional charge of a servant.

I.2.2- Requirement of mission warrants, mission orders or training decision

The special decree on civil servants travelling states explicitly that any travel on official business can only be done by virtue of application or decision by the competent authority. To this effect a mission warrant is issued for temporary movements, or a proof of a leave of absence, or transfer decision as regards transfers (decree n° 693/2000/PM of 13 september 2000).

a. The mission warrant

The mission warrant is established by the administration to which the public official reports, on a form issued by the ministry of Finance.

Mission warrants are signed by the competent authorities at the departure and arrival in the various administrative centres where the civil servant will stay. When travelling abroad, mission warrants are also signed at the entry and departure by the police of the airport and frontiers.

The public official concerned must ensure that statutory indications needed to assert that he is entitled to receive a daily compensation are written on the paper by each competent authority.

Departure and arrival time, accommodation and food supplied by the administration must be eventually specified. This information conditions the settlement of their rights and situation.

In the event of loss of his mission warrant, the public official must inform the competent authority who will issue a new one bearing the mention "*duplicate*". Statutory indications are recopied after the civil servant has signed a written statement under his responsibility.

b. Mission order within or abroad

A mission order for a civil servant may be established in two cases :

1. Firstly, in the name of the civil servant concerned for a mission within the country, decided by the head of the competent ministry.

The mission must be professional.

It includes the object, duration and itinerary of the mission.

It gives right to a mission warrant and transport requisition in the name of the civil servant. Transport charges may also be paid directly.

Temporary travel in this case entitles him to the exclusive payment of his personal transportation expenses within the national territory.

2. Secondly, the mission order may be established for a mission abroad.

Any official mission abroad must be authorized by the presidency of the Republic or the Prime minister's office, depending on the duties of the civil servant.

In case of violation of this requirement, disciplinary sanctions may be taken against him.

The mission order abroad entitles to a mission warrant and a voucher to take charge of the transport fare.

The minister who initiates the aforesaid mission may notably authorize the transportation of goods endorsed by the State during a mission abroad.

c. Decision authorising training course abroad

Public official travelling abroad for training courses lasting more than ninety (90) days are required to have an official decision signed.

This decision is signed by the minister of the public service. This implies that for less than ninety days, the prior accord of the minister is not needed.

Are the mission order and mission warrant sufficient in such a case ? As a matter of fact, many disputes arise to this effect.

d. Decision of assignment to a diplomatic mission

As provided for by the 2000 special rule (article 15), the posting or leave decision of a public official in a diplomatic or consular mission entitles the official to a mission warrant and a voucher to take charge of the transport fare.

It involves a change in the place of residence.

The aforementioned two documents are established by the minister of finance or the minister under whom the official works.

Transportation expenses are paid for the official, their spouse, dependent children, and one servant for heads of diplomatic missions.

The annual leave regime for these public officials is very restrictive.

The financial charges, are paid not only following regulators but also according to the availability of funds in the State budget. This may give rise to abuses and discrimination.

Transportation and travelling costs, including car transportation, are directly paid to the beneficiaries in case of transfer.

I.2.3. Travel advantages and allowances

The special provision on travels asserts the rights and structures the travel allowances granted to public servants.

a. Right to travel with luggage

a.1- Generalities

The right to transportation is most often stated.

The family of the public official, limited to the spouse and dependent children in the sense of the regulations on family allowances, is authorized to travel at the expenses of the administration, in the same class as the worker. Children under two (02) years, accompanied by their parents can travel by air in first class.

When travelling, the administration provides for the transport of the civil servant, and if need be, his luggage, either through his own means, by transport requisition or by hiring a vehicle.

Classes to which public officials can lay claim when traveling by train are divided into groups. Travelling by air within the country is reserved for civil servants of group I and II, namely those of categories 10 and 11, and civil servants classified at least at index 530.

The above mentioned, except heads of diplomatic missions, do travel by air in economy class.

a.2- Payment for leave

The state budget shoulders the transportation of workers when they go on their annual leave. Legislative, contractual or statutory provisions apply in this case within the limit of budget funds available (decree n° 693/2000/PM of 13 september 2000). This formulation is most ambiguous, as the application of law should not be subject to an individual decision linked to circumstantial changes. Only the employees concerned and their families are considered for transportation to and fro between the station and their place of origin.

These provisions also apply to civil servants and public workers who are on retirement.

a.3- Taking charge of postings

The travel expenses of public workers of diplomatic and consular missions transferred or on leave are assumed by the state.

The posting or leave decision causes a change of the place of residence.

The minister of finance and the minister to whom the civil servant reports both establish the mission warrant.

Transport expenses of the civil servant and his family –as termed by the social regulations-are covered, and that of a servant in addition for heads of diplomatic and consular missions.

In case of transfer, luggage transportation costs including the vehicle are paid directly to the civil servant.

Such costs are paid if the civil servant's transfer entails a change of place of residence.

a.4- Trainees transport requisitions

Public workers authorised by the government to study or take training courses abroad, are entitled to the payment of their transport to and fro.

On their return to Cameroon, the transport of the trainees' luggage by maritime freight is paid from the state budget within the limits of the authorized weight.

Public servants benefiting from a scholarship or being admitted to training courses cannot have their transport and luggage costs taken care of, if the transport of their luggage is paid for by international donors.

b. Allowances

Travelling may entail the payment of pecuniary benefits or allowances.

b.1- Mission allowances

Workers on mission abroad, classified by groups receive a daily allowance as mission expenses.

These allowances vary depending on the geographic area : Africa, Northern Africa, Southern Africa, Gabon, and Europe, except Austria, Switzerland, Pacific Asia, America and Oceania.

For reason of duty, a state worker may travel temporarily for a mission out of his duty station.

He can claim his personal transportation costs.

Depending on the case, a daily allowance is granted to the worker as mission fees for temporary displacements periodically. The travel must necessitate a temporary change of the professional residence.

This allowance is calculated according to the statutory classification.

b.2- Tour allowance within the national territory

There are daily and monthly allowances for tours.

1. A **daily allowance** may be granted as mission expenses to the worker on sporadic tours within the national territory. Such tours must involve a temporary change of residence for the worker. Such journeys are necessary for the exercise of his normal duties within his area of jurisdiction.

2. A **fixed monthly tour allowance** is granted to civil servants travelling within the national territory. They must, for duty obligations be frequently travelling within their territorial jurisdiction.

The aforementioned monthly allowance is granted on decision of the minister under whom the worker serves.

It is granted only during the exercise of those duties entitling them thereto and within the limit of votes intended for the payment thereof in the budget of the ministries concerned.

This travel allowance is paid on a quarterly basis following the commitment or order voucher, on presentation of a statement that recapitulates the tours record.

It is exclusive of the daily touring allowance within the territorial jurisdiction of the civil servant.

This allowance is usually granted to heads of administrative units : governors, senior divisional officers and divisional officers.

The allowance is paid in a lump sum, given that the number of tours cannot be determined. It is paid in compliance with the appendix of the instrument ruling administrative tours and defining statutory groups.

b.3- Allowance for lost items

Civilian personnel of the state who while on travel or transfer lose their belongings due to duly stated circumstances beyond their control, are entitled to an allowance for loss of belongings[1].

The allowance for lost items is decided by the minister of finance upon receiving a file comprising : a stamped application, a report of the loss by the competent authority ; a statement by the hierarchy of the civil servant certifying that the loss is relevant to service, and a detailed list of the lost items, possibly supported by corresponding bills.

The amount of the allowance is determined by the value of the lost personal effects within a maximum tariff determined in appendix III of the aforementioned instrument.

Jewellery, banknotes, and other paper money are not covered.

No allowance is consented if the loss is risk-covered by an insurance or was caused by mistake on the part of the civil servant.

b.4- Relocation allowance

Within the limit of one hundred (100) CFAF per kilogramme, the administration, with supporting evidence, refunds the moving costs occasioned by a transfer.

These costs consist in luggage fitting, packing, trucking and eventually parking and storage up to four (4) days.

b.5- Other allowances

Displacement may induce the payment of other allowances.

1. A daily allowance for temporary posting or transfer

Nevertheless, when accommodation and food are free of charge, no allowance is paid.

In this case, the allowance may be divided in two, not limited food charges, because the civil servant out of station must necessarily spend on more than just food and housing.

2. A daily allowance is given to the civil servant in case of posting. It is paid during a maximum period of one week.

---

[1] See article 7 of decree n° 2000/693 PM 13 september 2000.

The amount is reduced by half for the spouse, and three quarters (3/4) for each dependent child, if the family accompanies the civil servant or joins him.

It is worth noticing that transportation costs, in case of posting, can only be paid from the State budget once every three years for the same civil servant, except for service requirement.

This provision is difficult to understand, since a worker does not post himself. duty requirement is the only justification for his posting.

A civil servant posted for health reasons after consultation with the health board, takes charge of the related travel costs expenses himself.

Here is a provision just as hard to understand as the above mentioned, since health deterioration is usually a case of force majeure.

In conclusion, a transfer should not impose any additional financial burden on the worker without reason.

This is why it is stipulated that when the transport is not assumed by the administration, the worker can lay a claim for the reimbursement of his travel expenses by the State.

This reimbursement should be in accordance with the statutory classification of the civil servant, according to current transport rates, following the shortest itinerary from one place to another, duty station to the place of origin, duty place to the place of posting.

I.3- RIGHT TO A PENSION

As for the civil servant himself, all civil pensions are recorded in decree n° 74/759 of 26 august 1974. Another decree n° 78/788 of november 9, 1978 defines the conditions required to grant civil and military pensions, life annuities, death benefits and death allowance[1].

Other instruments govern[2] state workers. We shall mainly focus on the pension right of civil servants.

---

[1] See MINFOPRA, « Practical guide for retirement and the calculation of benefits », june 2007, 28 pages.

[2] See decree n° 92/221/PM of 8 may 1992 fixing the modes of admission to retirement of State agents governed by the Labour Code…
Order n° 0023 53/CAB/MFMRA of 24 may 1993 fixing the attribution and liquidation of payments…

Article 24 of the general rules and regulations recognizes the "right" of the civil servant "to pension".

Article 123 further declares : « *retirement shall mark the normal end of the active employment of the civil servant and shall entitle him to pension paid by the treasury or any other pension fund under conditions laid down by the president of the Republic* ».

Old-age pension is defined as "*a financial allowance granted, to some public servants in consideration of the services rendered until the regular termination of their duties*".

Who is entitled an old-age pension and what are the different types of pension ?

What is the legal regime, or rules applicable to the pension system ?

I.3.1- Rightful claimants and types of pension for the civil servant and legal heirs

Rightful claimants, rights and types of pension are determined by the law.

a. Rightful pension claimants

The 1994 general rules and regulations institute pension when the civil servant is on retirement. It is paid by the treasury or by any pension fund as underlined.

This right is admitted for the civil servant.

Pension is primarily for tenured civil servants of the public service, magistrates of the judiciary and permanent civil servants of the national security.

Secondarily, after the death of the rightful claimants, it is open to their legal successors, namely the surviving spouses entitled to a reversionary pension, children under 21, provided that they are not married, not salaried workers, and not yet emancipated.

Civil servants seconded to local councils and cameroonian public companies, foreign States or organizations regularly pay quarterly deductions to the public treasury, to which employers add a contribution equal to 12% of their remuneration calculated on the basis of their index.

Members of government or persons exercising official elective duties pay a 6% pension contribution calculated on the basis of their grade index.

The right to pension of the aforementioned persons who are on secondment or automatic secondment is conditioned by the payment of these deductions. The pension cannot be paid out for the period during which corresponding deductions were not deposited.

Civil servants entitled to statutory pensions are given a subscription booklet in which are mentioned : the surnames, first names, number, type and amount of pension and date of each payment.

Decision-employed workers, contract workers, temporary civil servants, and for now, local council staff do not benefit from pension.

The death and coming of age of some legal successors cause the loss of the right to pension. Validation rules of services adjust the types of pension to be paid to rightful claimants and legal successors.

b. Types of pension for civil servants

One must distinguish between pensions that derive from pension by seniority and the other ones.

b.1- Seniority pension

It is attributed to the civil servant who has fulfilled at least 25 years of effective service on the date of retirement, is aged fifty five (55) for civil servants of categories A and B, and fifty (50) for workers of categories C and D. Seniority pension can also be attributed to the civil servant dismissed without forfeiture of his right to pension, provided he had worked for twenty five (25) years.

The above required age can be reduced by one year for female civil servants on the account of each dependent child, the total of this benefit not exceeding three (03) years.

Seniority pension can also be approved for civil servants dismissed without cancellation or forfeiture of his rights to pension, if he has been working for twenty five (25) years entitling to pension. It can be paid immediately in case of early retirement, after twenty (20) years of effective service.

b.2- Proportionate Pension

The right to proportionate pension is attributed.

1. To civil servants who have attained the retirement age-limit, but do not qualify for seniority pension ;

2. Without the age or duty time requirement, to civil servants retired because of permanent disability acquired in the discharge of their duties or in the course of discharging their duties.

3. To civil servants who have been dismissed without forfeiture of their pension rights after twenty (20) years of service.

4. Female employees with at least three dependent children who have put in at least seventeen (17) years of service leading to pension.

Proportionate pension is considered when the 25 years of service normally required have not been performed.

b.3- Disability pension

In case of disability attributable to duty or an act of devotion accomplished in the public interest, a disability pension may be allocated to a civil servant.

The civil servant who becomes permanently disabled and totally unable to continue performing his duties as a result of a duly certified illness, injury or serious disability is automatically admitted to retirement. The retirement is declared at the end of the sick leave or of an extended sick leave pursuant to statutory provisions. When the cause of the disability is attributable to a third party, the state has the right to substitute for the victim or his rightful claimants and prosecute against the third party who is legally liable to reimburse the paid allowances.

The effectiveness of the disability, the extent, permanent disability to carry out duties and the evidence that the disability is attributable to duty are determined by the national health board or by the discharge centre and the armed force discharge committee as concerns the national security personnel. The decision lies in the hands of the appointing authority. The disability pension is added to the proportionate or seniority pension.

The degree of disability is determined using the Maillet scale (appendix 2) and the amount of disability pension is equivalent to the basic salary of the civil servant concerned multiplied by the degree of disability. A partial permanent disability duly certified by the national health board or the armed forces reforms centre induces the attribution of a proportionate disability pension.

The minister of state in charge of justice and the minister of finance have the right to substitute for the victim or his rightful claimants when they bring a suit against the third party for the reimbursement of paid allowances.

The disability pension cannot be reviewed except in the following instances :

- when a practical investigative error was made during the proceedings preparing the matter for judgment ;

- new disabilities become obvious or old disabilities have grown worse.

The retired civil servant can also benefit from disability pension cumulatively with seniority or proportionate pension when the disability is attributable to duty or to an accomplished act of devotion, when he is rightly on retirement.

The disability pension is equal to the gross indexed salary of the civil servant involved multiplied by the degree of disability.

b.4- reversionary pension for the civil servant's spouse(s)

The surviving spouse(s) of deceased civil servants are entitled to receive a reversionary pension corresponding to 50% of the old-age pension of the deceased, or that they might have obtained on the date of death and eventually increased with half of the disability pension which they deserve. Reversionary pension is calculated on the basis of seniority at the time of death if the civil servant died in active service without fulfilling the requirements qualifying him to a normal pension.

The amount of this pension should however not be less than that of a pension calculated on the basis of the basic salary paid for an equal number of years in service.

In case of polygamy, 50% of the old-age pension or disability pension is equally shared among the widows.

If one of the widows dies or remarries, her share is added to the minor orphans' or, in default, that of the other widows.

In case of monogamy, if the surviving spouse dies or remarries, her share increases the minor orphans' share.

A divorced spouse is not entitled to receive a reversionary pension. In this case, children are considered to be motherless and fatherless and only entitled to the children's pension.

b.5- Orphans' pension

Each orphan who does not earn a salary and is not married, has the right, up to the age of 21 years or until emancipation, to a reversionary pension calculated on the basis of the old-age pension eventually added to the disability pension the deceased obtained or might have obtained on the day he died, the total benefits allocated to the surviving spouse and to children not exceeding the amount of the pension granted or that might have been granted to the deceased.

50% of the pension is equally distributed among the orphans. The rate for each of them should not be less than the family allowances rates in force. A child, who no longer benefits from the pension due to death or coming to age, increases the share of the other children. Recognized, legitimate or adopted children are considered on the same level.

Children are entitled to the cumulated pensions of their deceased parents and eventually to the disability pension the deceased enjoyed or might have enjoyed.

In case of polygamy, only the children of the deceased female civil servant can benefit from both pensions of their father and mother.

Children's temporary pensions are paid to the surviving spouse or to the person taking care of the children, especially in case of death of the spouse or if the latter is unable to obtain a pension or has been waived of his right.

The surviving civil servant's spouse may select either a temporary orphan's pension or family allowances.

I.3.2- Fundamental rules of the pensions system

We will only mention the fundamental rules here below :

a. Conditions for granting pensions

"Any application for proportionate seniority pension or disability pension must, at the risk of forfeiture, be filed within four (04) years from

the date of departure on retirement and for the legal successors from the date of death of the civil servant or of the event necessitating the suspension of his pension."

Pension, whatever its nature, can thus be forfeited after four years.

Instruments laying down the retirement of civil servants are prepared one year in advance by competent authorities in accordance with the regulations.

Pensions are granted by the minister of finance and cannot be assigned or distrained.

They are recorded in the national expenditures register of the state and kept at the pensions' service within the salary department of the ministry of finance.

Before the 1st of january every year, a nominative statement per corps, rank and class of state workers to go on retirement is drawn up. This statement is drawn up by the minister of public service, the delegate general for national security and the minister of justice. It helps in establishing the expenditures on pension.

The granting of pensions, especially old-age pension, is subject to other rules : "civil and military pensions, life annuities and death benefits are thus granted :

- by enactment of the president of the Republic to the magistrates, staff of the national security, officers of the police and armed forces ;

- by order of the minister of armed forces as regards other staff of the armed forces ;

- by order of the minister of public service for workers governed by the general rules and regulations and contract workers ;

- by order of the minister of justice for civil servants ruled by the penitentiary administration ;

- by decision of user ministers or governors as concerns auxiliaries of the administration[1]".

---

[1] See decree n° 78-488 of november 9, 1978 defining the attribution of civil and military pensions, life annuities, death benefit and death allowance.

For workers employed on decision, the death allowance is granted by decision of the Ministers concerned, and for contract workers by decision of the Minister of Public Service[1].

It should be noted here that the minister of finance, the minister of state for justice, the minister of public service and the general delegate for national security are responsible for the implementation of the civil servants pensions system.

b Rules for raising the age-limits for pension applicants

Common provisions for seniority and proportionate pensions strictly regulate the rules defining the raising of age-limits.

They can be raised *intuitu personae* by one year per dependent child as regards the regulation on family allowances at the time of retirement.

The total prolongation should not be over 3 (three) years.

These limits can be raised in the interest of service and today the total extensions should not be over seven (07) years.

Besides, the number of extended age-limits granted every year to each corps is limited to 30% in category A, 20% in category B and 10% in category D.

These extensions do not affect the type of pension. They are not cumulative by reason of dependent children or in the interest of service.

c. Rules governing services taken into account

Time spent on release is not taken into account to qualify for pension. Only services rendered as a permanent civil servant as from 17 (seventeen) years on are taken into account. Duties during internships, provided they led to the payment of the 6% statutory deductions for pension, duly validated services of auxiliaries, temporary services by workers employed on decision accomplished as from seventeen (17) in the different services of the public administration of the Republic, services performed while on secondment as members of government or Parliament and services of the same nature performed in the former federal republic of Cameroon or former federated states of western Cameroon and Eastern Cameroon are considered. The validity of services

[1] Ibid.

is established by decision of the minister of finance after prior payment of the 6% legal deductions to the treasury.

The validation should be requested before retirement. It should be confirmed by a decision of the minister of finance after prior payment of the legal deductions to the treasury.

The deduction is calculated on the basis of the salary paid for the job position held at that period at the date of the request.

For a civil servant on probation, the rate of deductions is 6% of his indexed salary. In case he is not confirmed in his duties the deductions will be refunded to him.

d. Rules governing the calculation of pensions

To begin with a special and derogatory rule exists :

"The civil servant who resigned from duty, was laid off or dismissed and took up a public job entitling him to pension shall during his retirement benefit from all the services rendered before the termination of service" (article 15 of decree n° 47-747 of 24 august 1974).

The civil servant must return to the state budget the amount of deductions or the pension that might have been paid or refunded to him.

The calculation does not follow the standard procedure.

The duration of services considered for the calculation of pension is expressed in annuities calculated for seniority pension and is fixed at 38. It may rise to 45 if bonuses are taken into account. The annual growth of the seniority pension cannot exceed 90% of the basic annual indexed salary the civil servant was percerving at the time he was placed on retirement. Seniority or proportionate pension cannot be inferior to the annual indexed salary calculated on the basis of index 100. Family allowances restricted to family benefits are eventually added to the seniority or proportionate pension. In this regard, each child preserves the system that was his at the time of the retirement. A single birth allowance of 10.500 CFAF is granted for births occurring after retirement.

e. Special rules of the pension system

Two other rules play an important role : the rule of the non accumulation of pensions and the rule of the reimbursement of deductions.

e.1- The rule of non accumulation of pensions

Accumulating two or more old-age pensions or one of them with a remuneration paid by the state, local councils and companies, with indemnities gotten during the exercise of an elective duty is forbidden beyond five times the subsistence wage, except for the disability pension. If this limit is crossed, a deduction is made on the old-age pension.

The consequences of this rule of non accumulation are :

i) a compulsory declaration of any employment of a state pensioner by any local council, public or semi-public service paying the latter must be made to the minister of finance ;

ii) compulsion for the retired civil servant to present a certificate of duty or of non duty established by competent authorities every legal year ;

iii) restitution of wrongly collected sums, without prejudice to any penal sanctions, and the striking off of cheats from the national pensions register.

It would be also worthwhile noting that any local council, public or semi-public utility which pays a wage to a State pensioner for whatever reason must report same to the minister of finance within one month of his taking up employment with them (article 35 of decree n° 74/759 of 26 august1974).

e.2- Regulations for the reimbursement of deductions

The civil servant who is struck off from the staff for any reason and who is not qualified to benefit from pension, can benefit from the refund of the 6% deduction, calculated on the basis of the last three months index. In case of death, the refund shall be made to his heir. Deductions on this amount for the payment of government debts are probable. For that purpose, a written application must, at the risk of forfeiture, be submitted within the four (04) years following the termination of his appointment.

It should be noted that if the civil servant is indebted to the State, public corporations or companies, the debt must be collected from the refundable deductions.

I.4- THE RIGHT TO FUNERAL EXPENSES AND OTHERS

Article 127 of the 1994 general rules and regulations makes this point clear :

« *(1) the duties of a civil servant shall cease with his death*

(2) government shall bear all costs relating to the coffin and transportation of the mortal remains as well as all expenses relating to the laying in the coffin".

It should therefore be borne in mind that the rightful claimants of the deceased are entitled to claim the cost of transportation of the corpse.

The government purchases the coffin. It takes shoulders of the cost of transporting the mortal remains and laying it in the coffin ; the corpse is transported from the place of death to the place of burial.

Other charges are also paid :

« *It shall be responsible for the transportation of the legitimate spouses or spouse and minor children as well as their belongings from the place of posting of the deceased civil servant to the declared place of residence* » (article 127, paragraph 3).

A joint order of the minister of public service and the minister of finance defines the charges pertaining to the laying in the coffin of the deceased civil servant.

It was assumed that the administration supplies the coffin for the deceased retired civil servant. His legal claimants may demand the transportation of the corpse.

It should be noted that the government, on receipt of a statutory file, shall within three months pay the death benefits to the legal claimants.

Death as a result of accident attributable to duty or occurring in the course of duty leads to the payment of a fivefold death benefit. It seems to us the cameroonian government finds it difficult to respect the three (03) months delay.

II. OBLIGATIONS OF A CIVIL SERVANT AND THEIR SANCTIONS

The civil servant is subject to ethical behaviour and therefore, to obligations.

An obligation is meaningless unless it is accompanied by a system of sanctions.

What are the obligations of the civil servant ? And what is the legal system of the disciplinary sanctions inflicted to the civil servant ?

II.1- OBLIGATIONS OF THE CIVIL SERVANT

The obligations of civil servants are far from being just professional. They interfere with his life, especially his privacy.

II.1.1- Purely professional obligations

The civil servant must serve, obey and observe the ethical rules in force in the Public Service.

Article 35 of the 1994 general rules and regulations explicitly enumerates certain obligations :

- serve and be devoted to service ;
- abnegation ;
- obedience ;
- reserve ;
- professional discretion.

a. Obligation to personally carry out duties

The civil servant must occupy the position assigned to him, to which he was appointed. He must exercise his duties continuously, without interruption or slackening. He must be present at his duty post and personally carry out his duties.

The obligation to be devoted to his service is personal : the assignment of his duties must be spelled out by the texts.

He is answerable to his superiors for the authority conferred upon him and for executing orders received or ensuring the execution of orders given.

Appointment to duty posts is an innovation reinforcing this subordination and the obligation to personally carry out tasks that are within the remit of his “duty post”.

The 1994 general rules and regulations state : "*A civil servant shall be bound to personally perform the duties entrusted to him*" (article 36, paragraph 1).

This obligation to serve and entirely devote himself to his duties entails that he is not released from any of his responsibilities because of the responsibility of his subordinates, except for a personal fault they may commit.

b. Obligation to exercise duties exclusively and the prohibition of gainful activity

The civil servant must use his professional abilities exclusively to exercise his duties. Carrying out gainful activity is prohibited.

French administrative law prohibits the accumulation of public jobs paid from the budgets of local governments or national corporations.

However, a number of exceptions to this principle are permitted :

- civil servants can make consultations or offer their expertise to the Administration ;

- civil servants can teach subjects within their area of competence.

The general rules and regulations of the cameroonian public service do not maintain the express rule of the accumulation.

However, they undertake to ensure the exclusive exercise of duties and prohibit the carrying out of gainful activity.

"*A civil servant shall be bound to personally perform the duties entrusted to him and to devote himself thereto under all circumstances with diligence, integrity, respect for the state and a sense of duty*" (article 36, paragraph 1).

Any civil servant governed by the 1994 general rules and regulations is not authorised to :

"**i)** *possess..., in an enterprise or a sector under his direct control or in relation therewith, either personally or through an intermediary and under any title whatsoever, any interests likely to compromise his independence ;*

ii) *personally engage in* ***a private gainful activity****, except with special dispensation by an instrument*".

The prohibition does not apply to rural production, production of scientific, literary or artistic works, or teaching on a supplemental or temporary basis.

The civil servant must declare to the minister to whom he reports whenever his or her spouse exercises private gainful activity as a profession.

The administration shall, where and when necessary, eventually undertake measures liable to protect service interests.

Holding shares in the capital of public limited companies, privatized public corporations, rural production activities, and scientific, literary or artistic works is exempted and not subject to declaration.

Any default in declaring these activities of the spouse is a professional misconduct.

Is this prohibition total and "*erga totiae*" ?

Article 3 of decree n° 2000/691/PM of 13 september 2000 defining the conditions for the exercise of private gainful activity by civil servants is quite confusing :

« *A civil servant who engages in a private gainful non forbidden activity either personally or through an intermediary, must make a declaration thereof to the Minister under whom he is serving or to the one responsible for the organization of secondment, depending on the case* ».

The above mentioned activities are the only ones authorised : holding shares in the capital of rural production activities, scientific, literary or artistic works or teaching as a complementary activity.

Only the combination of several legal instruments in force (1994 general rules and regulations, decree n° 2000/691/PM of 13 september 2000, OHADA uniform act of 17 april 1997) can enable us to make a clear judgment.

The status of civil servant is incompatible with that of trader, particularly as regards :

- purchasing movable and fixed asserts for sale ;
- banking, stock exchange, brokerage, insurance or transit operations ;
- contracts between traders for trade purposes ;

- industrial exploitation of mines, quarries and natural resource deposits ;

- movable rental transactions ;

- factory, transport and telecommunications transactions ;

- intermediary transactions… ;

- operations carried out by trading companies.

The civil servant involved sends a declaration to the user minister and to the minister of public service relating to these activities incompatible with their status.

The ministers, if necessary, take appropriate measures to safeguard the interests of the service.

The declaration includes the following indications : first name, name, rank, official registration number and duty post. It also mentions the nature and title of the activity, whether it is a company, if so, the company name, the names and nationality of the manager, and a pledge on honour that he will devote only his free time for such activities and pay appropriate taxes promptly.

For a civil servant to use employees and movable and fixed asserts belonging to the state in pursuance of his private gainful activity is a professional misconduct.

In our opinion, the door left ajar by the latter provisions should be restricted to agricultural, artistic and scientific productions and lessons given as supplemental.

c. The duty of obedience towards hierarchy and the duty of disobedience

The duty to serve involves a duty of obedience towards hierarchy.

"Any civil servant is responsible for carrying out the tasks he is entrusted with. Consequently, he is bound to obey the individual and general instructions given by his service hierarchy in accordance with the laws and regulations"[1].

The requirement of compliance with legality is noteworthy.

What about obedience to illegal instructions ?

[1] Refer to article 39 of the general rules and regulations of the public service of 1994.

The duty of obedience is limited by the duty to respect the law. It is expressly stated in the general regulations :

"However, he has the duty to refuse an order that is manifestly unlawful and likely to seriously undermine public interest, except otherwise required by the competent authority under appropriate legal manner and procedures."

In this case, he is cleared of any responsibility. It is the same when he carries out legal instructions or instructions given as required by law.

The latter provision seems amazing. It substitutes his responsibility for that of the person who gave the order.

It can play in two extremes cases :

i) the order must be manifestly unlawful : case law may come to make an assessment in the event of assault or influence ;

ii) the order must be such as to seriously undermine public interest. Is public interest here limited to the safeguard of public order ? Does this mean that this order shall prevent a disturbance to the smooth functioning of public service ?

d. The obligation of professional discretion

"*Any civil servant must exercise professional discretion in all matters relating to facts, information or documents he had acquired in the course of or in connection with the performance of his duties.*" [1]

Only the authority under whom he works may release him from this obligation except in cases expressly provided for by existing laws.

This obligation of professional discretion goes beyond duties and is also required of the retired employee.

Moreover, "*any misappropriation or removal of official documents is strictly prohibited.*" It is the same for divulging or copying them, unless this is done for operational reasons and in the manner prescribed by the regulations in force[2].

[1] Refer to article 41 of the general rules and regulations of the public service of 1994, paragraph 1and 2.
[2] Ibid.

Cameroon administrative case law has endorsed this position (Judgement n° 27CS/CA of 29 january 1976, Diwouta Loth Martin versus the state of Cameroon).

e. The obligation of reserve

This requirement is for the civil servant to refrain from publicly expressing his political, philosophical, and religious or trade union opinions or serving according to such opinions.

A sharp boundary should be established with the right to enjoy his freedom of expression as an individual.

And this all the more as the general rules and regulations (article 21) have instituted duties requiring of their holders "loyalty to the institutions" of the Republic or "absolute political neutrality". This shall be the subject of a special enactment.

f. Other ethical obligations

The 1994 general rules and regulations retained other obligations under Article 36 :

- respect for public welfare ;
- a sense of responsibility.

It provides that he is also required to comply with requests for information, either from the public, or in response to queries from users. The "Aquarium" at the ministry of public service operates in this spirit of welcoming and informing users.

The sense of responsibility involves the internalization by the worker of the permanent need for accountability and service to users.

Objectivity is also an obligation of the civil servant on duty.

He must, under penalty of disciplinary sanctions, refrain from assessing his colleagues lightly or with bad faith.

And the superior is required to objectively assess the personnel placed under his guidance and authority[1].

These are statutory professional obligations predetermined by the general rules and regulations of 1994.

---

[1] Refer to article 43 of the general rules and regulations of the public service of 1994, paragraph 1and 2.

g. The duty of proper management

Law n° 74/18 of 5 december 1974 on the supervision of vote controllers, administrators and managers of public funds and State enterprises (as amended and supplemented by Law n° 76 / 4, 8 july 1976), requires of the civil servant a duty of proper management.

It applies to any public worker with a local council, state or para-statal institution or body in the capacity of a director of credit, auditor, censor or government commissioner with a state enterprise regardless of status, who is guilty of certain irregularities.

The civil servant or staff member involved then becomes a debtor to the corporation concerned of the amount of financial commitments not supported by documentary evidence. The following events shall be considered as irregularity and error of management prejudicial to the interests of the public :

- undertaking an expenditure without authority to do so or without having been delegated for this purpose ;

- undertaking an expenditure without available funds or designee ;

- undertaking an expense without sufficient documents ;

- undertaking an expenditure without a prior visa, authorization or requisition from the competent authority ;

- undertaking expenditure or certifying documents without justification of works, supplies of goods or services ;

- recruiting and actually employing a worker without the intervention of budgetary control when such control is prescribed by the regulations ;

- recruiting a worker in violation of existing labour regulations ;

- improper amendment of appropriations ;

- call for tenders, order letters and purchases made in breach of rules on public procurement ;

- use of employees or property belonging to the State and public authorities for personal gain where these benefits have not been granted by the laws and regulations.

The workers implicated are cleared of their responsibility if it is established that they acted on the written orders of their superior whose responsibility is thus substituted for theirs.

The budget and accounts disciplinary council reviews and rules on such irregularities.

It may be referred to by the president of the Republic, the minister in charge of state control and the supervisory ministers of the workers implicated or of the organs or institutions affected by irregularities.

On referral to the budget and accounts disciplinary council, its chairperson appoints a rapporteur who is qualified to conduct all useful inquiries and investigations. He can request the supply of any document and hear any witness.

At the opening of the hearing, the defendant is formally notified by all means with written proof of the decision to prosecute him.

He ensures his defence himself or by proxy. The council may, in case of non-appearance of the person duly summoned, go ahead and decide.

The board may impose a fine ranging from 200,000 to 2 million CFAF.

It can declare the defaulting public worker in debit, in proportion to the amount of the real prejudice incurred by the State or one of the interested public legal entities.

The fine and debit are eventually subject to an order of the minister in charge of state control.

The debit order is executed by the treasury to the benefit of the state or the interested public legal entity, who in such cases enjoy a lien.

Public institutions or organisations which do not enjoy this privilege proceed legally to recover sums due without the supervision of the Minister.

Decisions of the budget and accounts disciplinary council cannot be petitioned for reprieve.

A motion for annulment can be lodged before an administrative court without suspending recovery.

An application for reconsideration at the request of the defendant or the minister in charge of State control can be lodged before the council if new facts or documents are uncovered that call his guilt into question.

What happens if there is a breach of the duty of good management ?

Any civil servant found in default by the budget and accounts disciplinary council may incur one of the following forfeitures :

- A five year prohibition to hold office as a loan manager, authorizing officer or accountant in a department, para-statal corporation or state-owned enterprise ;

- Or prohibition to be responsible in any capacity whatsoever during five to ten years, of the administration or management of government services or state-owned enterprises.

It should be noted that ministers and secretaries general can not be brought before the budget and accounts disciplinary council.

Law n° 74/18 of 5 december 1974 is not exhaustive on the matter of duty of good management.

The Penal Code (Law n° 77/23 of 6 december 1977) defines other offenses and reinforces the obligation of good management of the civil servant.

Such offenses are numerous.

Article 184 punishes **embezzlement,** defining it as anyone who by any means whatsoever, fraudulently obtains or retains any assert, whether movable or fixed, belonging to, intended for or entrusted to the state, a cooperative, a community or a public institution or under the administrative supervision of the State or in which the state directly or indirectly holds a majority stake.

Article 134 punishes **corruption** with a prison sentence of 5 to 10 years and a fine of 200,000 to 2 million CFA francs, against any civil servant or any public official who, for himself or for another person, solicits, approves or receives offers, promises donations or gifts to perform, or refrain from performing or postpones an act that constitutes part of his duties. The prison sentence is 1 to 5 years and the fine 100,000 to one million CFA francs. Article 134 bis has reinforced the repression of corruption. It extends it to the performance, adjournment, abstention from any act, the obligation of a promise, offer, gift or present or yielding to the solicitations aimed at corruption. Past abstention is also punished. The crackdown extends to both the major actor and the briber.

Article 135 of the penal code punishes **interest in performing an act**, that is any public or civil servant who directly or indirectly receives an interest in acts or adjudications submitted to his approval or for which he is in charge of the survey, control, certification or award. The ban extends to private enterprises, cooperatives, para-statal companies, with financial participations of the state, state-controlled agencies, concessions under the surveillance or control of the civil servant. This also involves contracts, transactions with an individual or a legal entity in the name of the government or a public authority. It also extends to businesses for which he is in charge of ordering the payment or liquidating.

These provisions shall still be applicable, five (5) years after termination of activities in case of resignation, layoff, retirement release or any other cause.

That article prohibits any civil servant from having an interest either by himself or by proxy.

The term « *civil servant* » is here understood in the broadest sense of the penal code.

Article 136 of the same code also punishes **participation in a business** : the said civil servant is punished for participation in the activities or funding of any company, authority or concession.

Hereditary devolvement of capital relieves him of that responsibility.

The civil servant must not be in charge of supervising the enterprise. The ban is applicable even if he does not gain anything from the enterprise.

The ban also applies to retired civil servants or to those on release.

Article 137, on its part, punishes **concession**, that is a civil servant granting exemptions from duties, taxes, fees, levies or contributions, one that delivers a price lower than that prescribed for products of the State, cooperative, local council or institution... submitted to the administrative supervision of the State or in which the state directly or indirectly holds a majority stake.

The penal code punishes the **unreported deficit** with a prison sentence of one to five years. It consists in the fact that a civil servant who, having knowledge of a causal deficit or accounting deficit in the management of a worker under his command or supervision, fails to give notice thereof to the nearest judicial authority or his superior.

There are other related articles (95, 134, 144, 148, 151, 160, 161, 205, 207, 254 and 310) for various offenses : compelling civil servant, influence peddling, forgery, favouritism, false declarations, falsification of public accounts, writing of false official certificates, violation of freedom of auction professional secrecy, refusal of a due service, systematic carelessness, complicity within the meaning of the penal code, conspiracy, coercion and complicity.

II.1.2- Obligations in the civil servant's private life

The obligations of good management cross the boundary of privacy. Other obligations, although not expressly stated by the 1994 general rules and regulations of the public service, are nevertheless implicit in the private life of a civil servant.

They are :

- the general respect for the state and legality ;

- the eventual obligation of residence for civil servants of sovereignty ;

- the implicit obligation of dignity.

a. Obligation of respect for the state and legality

The civil servant is bound to respect the state and public order.

He is not above the law. The status of a civil servant does not exempt him from respecting the Constitution and the law outside service.

He may engage his own responsibility in case of assault (FJ order n° 8 of 16th october 1968 Federated State of East Cameroon versus Max Keller Ndongo).

Personal offence, assault or loss of self-control, respectively engage the responsibility of the civil servant concerned. It must be differentiated from service and in this matter only the judge is competent.

The responsibility may be assumed by the government, in case of personal misconduct in the course of duty. He may also engage his disciplinary responsibility at any moment for violating legality and the regulations in force.

Any dereliction, attitude or behaviour questioning the ethical and professional deontology or likely to undermine the public morals, can lead to the commission of a "***non- professional offence***".

Such acts or their mere presumption may prompt the government to take conservatory measures against the civil servant concerned.

b. Obligation of good repute

The former general rules and regulations expressly prescribed that the private life of a civil servant should not involve « any scandal or notable misconduct ». This formula had a rather broad meaning.

Such is no longer the case today. However the obligation of dignity or respectability still exists.

A "non-professional fault" can undermine the respectability of the public service. It may be caused by a dereliction, an attitude or behaviour that put ethics into question.

The government may take conservatory measures to this effect against the civil servant.

The analysis of the legal status of a trainee, implicitly confirms the existence of an obligation of dignity because only a "**morally upright"** worker on internship can become a civil servant.

We can therefore deduct *a contrario* and *a priori* that the applicant with ***bad character*** cannot be a civil servant.

Even then measures should be taken to decide whether to dismiss him or maintain him.

The obligation of dignity or respectability goes together with the other obligations of the civil servant, in particular those of abnegation, probity, good governance and the rule of law which constitute a real code of ethics and life.

c. Eventual obligation of residence

Is a civil servant obliged to reside in the place where he was posted ?

This obligation expressly exists only for a certain number of high officials, namely : heads of jurisdiction, heads of diplomatic missions abroad, high-ranking military officers, magistrates, treasurers, paymasters general…

For that category an authorization of the minister under whom they depend is required : the minister in charge of territorial administration for heads of jurisdictions, the minister of defence for military officers and commanders…[1]

The above ministers are also led to regulate the issues of residence of married couples.

When two (2) civil servants belonging to the same administration and residing in the same locality are married, their minister must choose the locality where they will be closer while taking into account service requirements, the family status and health condition as stated by medical certificates.

If both married civil servants belong to different administrations and reside in the same locality, the ministers on whom they depend are bound to give them a position matching their qualifications, in the locality where the husband works, or in the locality where the wife works according to the wish of the couple.

The cameroonian government is willing to preserve the family unit.

Up till now, from succession of states, only the Roustan law of december 20, 1923 amended by that of 4th june 1970 could be referred to. To move closer, the wife was posted to the division where the husband was on duty or to bordering communes. To this effect the French administration reserved 21% of vacant positions each year.

In the whole, there is a compulsory obligation of residence for civil servants. Married couples must be brought together only by reason of service requirements in a position equivalent to their qualification.

II.2- LEGAL REGIME OF DISCIPLINARY SANCTIONS

Three (03) main questions seem essential as regards disciplinary sanctions to inflict on civil servants :

What prompts the disciplinary sanction ?

---

[1] A senior divisional officer of the ocean department was relieved of his duties in the years 2000/2004.

What does the disciplinary sanction consist of and moreover which are the sanctions likely to be taken against the defaulting civil servant ?

II.2.1- Extensive conception of the disciplinary offence

Is the principle « *nullum crimen, nulla poena sine lege* »[1] valid in disciplinary administrative law ?

Criminal Law does not provide for incrimination or sanction without law.

The enumeration of disciplinary sanctions of the civil servant is limited and clearly expressed in cameroonian administrative law[2] :

- failure to assess his personnel ;

- assessing them without due care or in bad faith ;

- unduly benefiting from an extended sick leave ;

- non reinstatement within one month to a vacancy made available for a civil servant at the expiry of his secondment period... ;

- refusal to re-establish all the benefits of a suspended civil servant by his superior.

The above cases are expressly restrictively enumerated.

However the 1994 general rules and regulations of the public service extensively provide for disciplinary sanctions.

It is stated in article 92 : « *The civil servant shall be subjected to a set of rules and regulations which if violated constitute an offence, making him liable to disciplinary sanctions* ».

Further in article 93 :

"An offence may be professional or non-professional..."

A professional offence specifically is "*an advertent, inadvertent or negligent dereliction of the duties and obligations binding the civil servant*" (paragraph 2).

A non-professional offence particularly results from « *a dereliction, an attitude or behaviour which jeopardizes professional ethics or is such*

---

[1] Refer to the French Penal code, article 1113.

[2] Refer to the 1994 general rules and regulations, articles 43 (paragraph 2), 65 (paragraph 3) 76 (paragraph 3), 109 (paragraph 3).

that it is a breach of public morals or the respectability of the public service » (paragraph 3).

The disciplinary offence, professional or non- professional offence is thus defined in its broadest sense…

Everything is reviewed : dereliction, attitude, abstention, behaviour, negligence…

A professional offence is linked to duties and obligations that a civil servant must observe.

A non-professional offence is of an ethical and deontological nature, likely to breach public morals or the respectability of the public service.

It is worth noticing that a disciplinary offence does not fall under a criminal sanction or that resulting from a ruling by a judicial or legal officer or the disciplinary and accounting council.

The same disciplinary offence may not receive sanctions twice (2).

Hierarchical authorities dispose of a power of reformation of sanctions by their personnel against their collaborators.

A decision of a disciplinary sanction may be made public. The publication is of right in case of dismissal.

Any sanction must be motivated and any decision inflicting a disciplinary sanction is included in the personal file of the concerned.

The petition against a disciplinary sanction does not suspend its execution and effects except in the case of suspension of the execution approved by the judge, and except any contrary provision of the law.

II.2.2- Types of disciplinary sanctions

The 1994 general rules and regulations provide four (4) groups of sanctions. How far do they have an impact ?

a. Groups of sanctions

There are four groups of disciplinary sanctions :

i) Sanctions of the first group include the written warning and the reprimand to be recorded in the file of the civil servant ;

ii) Sanctions of the second group go from the deferment of increment for a one year period to the reduction of one or two incremental positions ;

iii) Sanctions of the third group consist in the reduction in class, the temporary suspension from duty for a period less or equal to six months ;

iv) Sanctions of the fourth group only involve dismissal.

Sanctions must be based on motives, without which they are declared null and void. They are obligatorily recorded in the professional file of the civil servant.

b. Impact of disciplinary sanctions

Disciplinary sanctions may affect wages and advancement in grade and duties.

b.1- Sanctions affecting the salary

Temporary suspension entails the suspension of the civil servant's salary concerned for the duration of the sanction, but not including, if they exist, family allowances. Deductions for pensions are not to be suspended.

b.2- Sanctions deferring advancement

Deferment of advancement relates to the advancement in incremental position, class or grade.

Reduction in incremental position entails the deduction of one (1) or two (2) incremental positions at most.

In both cases, the seniority required to be proposed again for advancement is prolonged by one more year.

The duration of the deferment of advancement takes effect from the date when the civil servant has gathered all the evaluation and seniority conditions required for advancement.

b.3- Demotion

Reduction in class or grade consists in returning the civil servant to the class or grade immediately below, provided it does not consequently cause a change in grade because of reduction in class or a change of cadre because of reduction in grade.

In any case the civil servant concerned by the reduction in class is returned to the first incremental position at the first stage of his class and can not be promoted before four (04) years. The civil servant concerned by the reduction in grade is returned to the first incremental position of his grade and can not be promoted for six (06) years.

b.4- Sanctions affecting duties

The written warning is a warning addressed to a civil servant ordering him to carry out his professional obligations in compliance with the regulations in force.

The reprimand recorded in the personal file is an admonishment to the civil servant for his performance and behaviour found wanting.

The above two measures may result in the reduction of assessment marks :

- by two (02) points when it is a written warning ;

- by four (04) points when it is a reprimand to be recorded in the personal file.

Demotion « *downgrades* » the civil servant who has to carry out duties in the grade immediately below, this should not result in a change in grade because of reduction in class, and change in cadre because of the reduction in grade.

Dismissal is a measure of total exclusion of the civil servant from the corps to which he belongs.

The minister of public service or the Prime minister, depending on the case, orders it.

Temporary cessation of service is the situation of the civil servant who is absent without leave or in custody.

Any breach of the obligation of effective presence in service without justification shall be considered as unauthorised absence as provided by the general rules and regulations, except in case of force majeure duly motivated.

Any absence without leave for at least thirty (30) consecutive days is considered as desertion of post.

It entails an automatic dismissal.

In addition, suspension from duty is a conservatory measure which produces a definitive effect only following a sanction taken by the competent authority. The civil servant is forbidden to come to his place of duty as long as the suspension lasts. He is deprived of his basic salary.

His situation must be re-established within four (04) months, failure of which may constitute a disciplinary offence for his immediate superior.

Temporary cessation of service may be consecutive to a detention. It is declared by decision of the minister of public service who reports to the minister of finance. The latter takes conservatory measures.

During the period of detention, the civil servant whose cessation of service has been confirmed loses his right to the indexed salary as well as various allowances and benefits. The full family allowances, if any, are still preserved.

The situation of the civil servant concerned who cannot carry out his duties is definitely settled only after the measure of detention has been lifted or the final decision of the court delivered.

II.2.3-Disciplinary procedure

It is convenient to establish the hierarchy of disciplinary authorities and distinguish the two (02) types of disciplinary procedure.

a. Hierarchy of competent disciplinary authorities

The disciplinary power belongs to the authority invested with the power of appointment or to the senior authority.

Except for disciplinary sanctions of the first group, the senior authority exercises the disciplinary power after approval of the permanent disciplinary council of the public service. He is habilitated to publish the decision for motive-based sanction.

The delegation of authority to make appointments embodies disciplinary power.

Still, the disciplinary power may be delegated separately for sanctions of the first group, namely, the written warning and reprimand recorded in the personal file.

The 1994 general rules and regulations established a hierarchy of authorities empowered to impose disciplinary penalties :

1. Secretaries-general of ministries, directors of the central administration, divisional officers, Sub-divisional officers, regional delegates, and in case the latter do not exist, regional service heads inflict sanctions of the first group ;

2. Sanctions of the first and second group are inflicted by the governor of the region, that is besides the written warning and reprimand, the deferment of advancement for a one (01) year period, the reduction in one or two (02) incremental positions ;

3. Ministers concerned and secretaries of State may in addition, inflict sanctions of the third group, reduction in class, and exceptionally temporary suspensions not exceeding six (06) months ;

4. The minister of public service imposes sanctions of the first, second and third group, namely all other sanctions, excluding dismissal ;

5. Dismissal may be decided, either by the minister in charge of the public service or the Prime minister, head of government in compliance with the provisions of the law. In this case, the decision is left to the authority who makes appointments.

Besides, the superior exercising disciplinary power is also authorized to impose sanctions within the competence of the disciplinary authorities who are under him.

He is also empowered to reform disciplinary sanctions taken by the latter.

The minister of public service and the minister of finance each receive a copy of the sanction decision taken by the governor, the ministers concerned or the Prime minister.

There is some decentralisation operating to the benefit of the user ministers, the heads of bordering jurisdictions and the organs participating in the management of civil servants career, such as the permanent disciplinary council.

b. Consultation of management organs of the public service : the permanent disciplinary council and the higher council of the public service

There are two (02) organs which play a major role in matters of discipline : the permanent disciplinary board and the higher council of the public service.

b.1- Consultation of the permanent disciplinary council.

This council has its headquarter in Yaounde. Regional councils may be created, if need be, by decision of the minister of public service.

The minister of public service or his representative is the chairman. The director in charge of disciplinary affairs, the director in charge of State personnel in the same ministerial department, the director in charge of salaries at the ministry of finance, the official in charge of human resources in the ministry concerned and one staff representative stand as members. The director in charge of career management has replaced the director of personnel. The staff representative is selected among the members elected at the joint administrative commissions having at least an equal grade.

The decision of the minister of public service on suing the sanctioned civil servant to the permanent disciplinary council requests a post deliberations report.

The secretarial duties of the council are assumed by the service in charge of disciplinary affairs of the ministry of public service.

The tasks are of significant importance :

- centralize and actualize files to be submitted to the council ;

- prepare the suing decisions council ;

- transfer the decisions and the disciplinary file to the chairman ;

- write and transmit, on instructions of the chairman, of individual invitations to council members ;

- follow-up, in relation with the minister of finance, the application of sanctions with a financial impact on the salaried worker ;

- transmit the council recommendation to the authority habilitated to take the sanction.

The permanent council is convened, when need arises, by its chairperson. The enrolled affairs, date, time and place of the meeting are indicated on the invitation letter.

The opinion of the council is communicated at the end of a secret ballot. Council members answer the question of the chair by writing yes or no on their ballot.

The council takes the decision at the single majority. In case of a tie, the chairperson has a casting vote. To this effect the chair ensures his ballot bears a special sign.

It should be underlined that the disciplinary procedure now operates by jurisdictions, this representing a guarantee of the rights of the civil servant concerned.

1. The minister of public service informs the council by a decision, clearly indicating the offence, the circumstances in which it was committed and the sanctions incurred.

The minister may instruct it on the initiative or request of one of the authorities invested with sanctioning powers…

2. On receiving the act, the chair of the council transmits it to the rapporteur together with the suing file, against an acknowledgment notice.

The above file must necessarily include all documents related to the charges against the civil servant (his written explanations), any decision on previous sanctions, opinions and recommendations of various disciplinary councils.

3. On receiving the file, the rapporteur informs the civil servant by any written means.

The transmitted file must contain all the documents, the civil servant must be informed of every document containing a disciplinary motive to enable him valuably defend himself.

The concerned must certify that the case was forwarded to him.

Forwarding the case file in totality is a "*substantial formality*" whose non observance may entail cancellation of the procedure. This rule is constantly applied (affair Baba Youssoufa versus the State of Cameroon, order n° 9 of october 16, 1968).

« *Attendu que Baba Youssoufa aurait dû obligatoirement être avisé de la décision n° 36 du 12 février 1965 de Monsieur le Premier Ministre le traduisant devant la commission de qualification pour savoir les griefs qui étaient articulés contre lui, invité à comparaître devant elle, mis en demeure de prendre communication intégrale de son dossier personnel pour lui permettre de se défendre, entendu par la Commission assisté le cas échéant d'un défenseur de son choix »*[1].

The concerned must have been forwarded his file and been informed of his hearing by the board.

4. The rapporteur plays one of the most active roles.

He must **show proof of absolute impartiality**. He has to seek with equal care the elements most favourable for the case of the accused and those which may confirm the charges against the accused, adopting a benevolent attitude towards him as well as witnesses, not hinder, through intimidation manoeuvres the truth from prevailing.

He acts as an examining magistrate and has a thorough knowledge of the disciplinary file.

He proceeds to make investigations, inquiries and research helpful to know the truth.

He has access to all documents necessary for the instruction of the case and hears every person likely to clarify some details.

He may also request any competent administrative or judiciary authority, to establish a minute report intended for the council, by examining all the persons needed to be heard.

He collects statements of the civil servant's parents, relatives and friends, only for information purpose.

The rapporteur, after concluding his inquiry, produces a report whose conclusions sum up the grievances retained and those rejected. Evidences supporting his view are necessarily appended to the report.

The defendant is only informed of the content of the report during the council session. At the end of the investigations the rapporteur transmits it, against acknowledgment of receipt, with the complete disciplinary file to the chair.

5. The civil servant who is accused sees his rights to defence recognized and consolidated.

He is invited by all written means to go through the accusation file.

---

[1] Refer also to the affair MPESSA Stanislas vs. the State of Cameroon, order n° 11 of october 18, 1967.

A staff representative selected among elected members at the Joint administrative board having a rank at least equal to that of the accused civil servant sits at the permanent council.

The file must be complete.

A summons is addressed to the concerned indicating the matters filed at the session, date, time and place of the sitting.

The opinions of the council have to be based on motives.

Every sitting of the council is minuted and the minutes are signed by all members present.

This is a contradictory procedure where the concerned has the right to contradict the accusations made against him.

Testimonies are recorded and countersigned by the person who states facts.

The accused may plead himself for his defence. He may be assisted at his own expenses by a lawyer or any other proxy of his choice. He may also chose witnesses for his cause.

Then the decision suing him to the council is read to him.

He must then pronounce that he has no more statement to make. At this point, it is no more possible to complain or contest the legality of the proceeding on relevant documents unknown to him contained in the file (case Onana Jean Pierre versus the State of Cameroon, order n° 3 of october 28, 1970).

He may, on authorization of the chair of the council question and cross-examine witnesses, a procedure inspired from the cross examination of Common Law.

The accused is the last one to take the floor and plead for his defence.

The chair informs the concerned of sanctions incurred by him.

6. Meanwhile, the chair actively conducts the procedure :

- he transmits the introductory file to the rapporteur ;

- he receives the investigated and closed file from the rapporteur ;

- he sends personal invitations to the members of the Board, the accused and any other person likely to provide information ;

- he refers to the minister of public service as regards facts reported to him, different from those listed in the proceedings decision.

- he opens the session of the permanent council, has the accused and his counsel introduced in the room, reads the suing decision ;

- he gives the floor to the rapporteur, requires the accused to make observations and witnesses their depositions ;

- members are authorized by the chair to ask questions to the accused or his counsel ;

- he closes hearings by reminding to the members the charges against the accused as specified in the decision.

On request of the chairperson members vote a disciplinary sanction, starting with a minor one.

7. The opinion of the council is released under special conditions.

It is the result of a secret ballot. The council pronounces the sanction at the single majority of members with a casting vote for the chair in the event of a tie. His ballot then bears a distinctive sign.

Each council member answers by yes (positive answer) or no (negative answer) by writing his answer on a ballot dropped inside a ballot box.

The council sessions are not public. Opinions expressed must be based on evidences in respect of the right to defence.

Each session is minuted, copy of the minutes is filed in the council archives.

It is signed by all the members present.

The accused is not informed of the result. The minutes are transmitted to the minister of public service.

This is in the case where the suing initiative was taken by another authority vested with such a disciplinary power.

A copy of the decision is addressed to the minister of public service and the minister of finance.

Failure to obey a subpoena or take information is considered as a contempt by the council which further proceeds, ruling by default.

Duties as president, member, rapporteur or secretary during council sessions are free.

However, the above mentioned may receive a session allowance and payment of their transport and travel expenses.

The chair is entitled to receive an allowance of 150,000 Cfaf, member 100,000 Cfaf, rapporteur 50,000 Cfaf, and secretary 25, 000 Cfaf per file.

The amount of the allowance per session is fixed by a special rule.

The council's running costs are assumed by the budget of the ministry of public service.

The authority with disciplinary power is not bound by the opinion of the council (Moukoko James vs. the State of Cameroon, decision n° 14 of march 19, 1969) :

« Mais attendu que l'Administration apprécie souverainement la sanction à prendre dans le cadre de l'échelle des peines prévues par les textes.

Que d'autre part, elle n'est pas tenue de suivre l'avis émis par le Conseil de discipline.

Qu'en l'espèce, le Conseil ayant émis l'avis que Moukoko devait être rétrogradé, l'Administration pouvait légalement prononcer la révocation, cette sanction figurant à l'échelle des peines fixées par le statut de la Fonction publique ... ».

Hence the opinion does not bind the State. The decision must not necessarily be right. The authority invested with disciplinary power appreciates in all sovereignty.

b.2- Consultation of the higher council of the public service.

The higher council of the public service is defined as a consultative management organ of the public service, acting as an advisory organ to the government and a participatory organ regarding civil servants. It is acknowledged for its competence in all projects related to the condition of civil servants, issues on their rights and obligations and any amendment project of the general rules and regulations[1].

---

[1] See decision n° 2000/698 of september 13, 2000 organizing the functioning of the highest council of the public service, article 2 (paragraphs 1 and 2).

It rules moreover on petitions mostly in cases of : "suspension for a period over four months, demotion in class or grade, dismissal from service for professional incompetence".

The council gives opinions or makes recommendations that are not certified and not binding for the authority of decision.

However it would be suitable to recall that the highest council of the public Service is a high organ presided over by the Prime minister, head of government, composed of over nine members of government[1] coming from various ministerial departments.

The civil servant incriminated addresses a request referral to the highest council of the public service to the Prime minister.

Staff representatives at the higher council of the public service are elected by single round, single majority ballot for three years, renewable twice (02).

The election is witnessed by the minister in charge of the public service.

The public service commission for claims prepares petition files introduced by civil servants against penalties such as : temporary suspension of service, dismissal for professional incompetence or demotion in class or grade, for the attention of the plenary assembly of the higher council of the public service.

The procedure is almost similar to the consultation of the permanent disciplinary council :

1. The president and members of the commission are selected by the president of the council, the Prime minister, head of government ;

2. A rapporteur is appointed by the president among members to investigate the case. He shall not have any prior knowledge of the case before filing at the secretariat of the council. He has investigation power to the relevant administrations and must seek with the same care all elements favourable to the incriminated civil servant as those likely to confirm the charges against him.

---

[1] See article 4 of decree n° 2000/698 of september 13, 2000 fixing organizational modes and functioning of the highest board of the public : public service, finance, territorial administration, education, justice, social affairs, labour, supreme State audit, women's affairs,

The rapporteur casts a complete light on the affair. He is neither the advocate of the Administration nor of the accused[1]. He is instead a kind of commissioner for legality and truth.

He writes a report and the council must give an opinion within six months starting from the date of introduction of the file :

- the opinion must be based on motives and the case is reviewed in plenary assembly ;

- files brought before the higher council of the public service cannot suspend other claims.

Duties of members of the highest council of the public service are not remunerated. They are however paid a session allowance, and transport and travel expenses are reimbursed.

A special provision determines the amounts of allowances, of the president (150,000 Cfaf), member (100,000 Cfaf), rapporteur (50 000 Cfaf) and the session secretary (25,000 Cfaf).

c. Types of procedure per se

At this point a distinction may be made between accelerated and ordinary procedures mainly governed by the above mentioned regulations.

c.1- Disciplinary procedure accelerated by suspension

Article 145 of the former rules and regulations declared that in case of serious offence committed by the civil servant, be it a breach of professional obligations, a misdemeanour under common law or participation in subversive activities, the civil servant who committed the offence could be temporarily suspended one to three months by the minister under whom he served, who immediately informed the minister of public service and forwarded the disciplinary file of the civil servant to him within one month.

If after three (3) months of suspension, no disciplinary decision was taken, the suspended civil servant was reinstated in his job position.

He would lose the right to his basic salary but still keep his entire allowances. He could retroactively recover his total rights.

The above description is an accelerated disciplinary procedure.

---

[1] See TEKAM, *Fonction publique camerounaise, Op cit..*, p. 245.

This provision was replaced by article 108 of the 1994 general rules and regulations which sounds more liberal as regards deadlines (four months), and basically resumes the former provision :

« In the event of a serious offence committed by a civil servant relating to a breach of professional duty, an ordinary law offence or a breach of professional ethics, the author of such offences may be provisionally suspended from his duties for not more than 4 (four) months by the minister under whom he is serving. The latter shall forthwith inform the minister in charge of the public service and forward to him the disciplinary file made in respect of the accused within a period not exceeding one month ».

The sanction must have been pronounced after four months, failure of which the civil servant is fully reinstated in his job position.

The government is only habilitated to take conservatory measures. What about sanctions ?

Still we can assert that this disciplinary measure, while affecting the salary –a right- of the civil servant, seems to be in fact a disguised disciplinary procedure, but accelerated by the conservatory measure.

Upon referral of the sanctioned civil servant, the administrative judge is habilitated to verify and appreciate the seriousness of the fault having caused the suspension of duty.

Meanwhile there has been a positive development : subversion was crossed out from the list of faults likely to cause suspension.

c.2- Ordinary disciplinary procedure

The ordinary disciplinary procedure essentially follows rules already mentioned : the appearance before the permanent disciplinary council, conduct of the session by the president, defence rights guaranteed to the civil servant, decision taking, and effect of the opinion…

This time there is no previous suspension of work or conservatory measures. The suspension is not pronounced before the final decision.

There are a number of rules to be reminded :

- consultation of the permanent disciplinary council is a significant formality (CFJ/CAY order n° 121 of december 8, 1970 Sitamze Urbain versus the State of Cameroon). Constant case law on the part of the Cameroonian administrative judge (Baba Youssoufa versus the State of

Cameroon, decision n° 9 of october 16, 1968 and Mpessa Stanislas vs. the State of Cameroon, decision n° 11 of 18 october 1967) ;

- the accused must, at the behest of the rapporteur, go through his file and the charges against him (article 16 of decree n° 2000/685 of september 13, 2000) ;

- the civil servant may ensure his defence, be assisted by a counsel at his own expenses, or any other proxy of his choice, and call witnesses to defend his cause ;

- the concerned must expressly declare that he does not have anything to add at the end of the debates ;

- opinions expressed by the permanent disciplinary council are based on motives and sessions are not public ;

- the civil servant must be informed of the disciplinary sanction.

The rules in force have also instituted a rehabilitation procedure.

The effect is to lift the heavy shackle that the sanction put on the career of the civil servant (advancement). It automatically wipes out the sanction in his personal file.

His advancement is to be continued. It does not result in career reconstruction or remuneration arrears.

For the above conditions to be fulfilled, the following is required :

- the civil servant must specifically make a request ;

- the measure is taken by the competent authority who also has the power of appointment ;

- no other sanction must have been imposed on the civil servant at the end of two years for written warning, three years for reprimand, five years for any other sanction, except dismissal.

III. PROTECTION OF THE CIVIL SERVANT

The civil servant needs to be protected, not only as regards citizens, but also and perhaps mainly as regards the State, his all mighty employer.

III.1- PROTECTION OF CIVIL SERVANTS VIS-A-VIS CITIZENS

The civil servant here has two (02) types of guarantees : penal guarantee through particular sanctions against those who commit offences against civil servants and granting of special guarantees on contentious matters.

III.1.1- Penal protection of the civil servant

The general rules and regulations set the principle, while the penal code arranges it.

a. Protection principle

Article 25 of the 1994 general rules and regulations states : « *the State shall be bound to protect civil servants against threats, contempt, assault, interference, abuse or defamation to which they may be exposed by reason of or during the performance of their duties* ».

The above basic provision entails several consequences in law :

After having due assessment, the State is bound to repair any damages sustained by the civil servant as a result of such acts.

i) The State automatically stands in for the victim in order to have the incriminated refund the amounts and other expenses paid to the civil servant in compensation for damages incurred.

ii) The State may also prosecute the offenders. It may sue the offender in penal court, that is, the victim of a penal infraction bringing a lawsuit in compensation for the damage caused. It can also bring criminal charges against the perpetrators, instrumental to the repair of damages for a victim of a crime. This action sets the prosecution in motion.

b. Penal provisions of the protection

The cameroonian penal code clearly prescribes a number of offenses in order to efficiently ensure the penal protection of civil servants and punish the perpetrators.

b.1- Insult to civil servants

Contempt of the president of the Republic or officials is punishable by a jail sentence of one to five years (article 153). Any one who insults, courts and tribunals, armed forces, constituted corps and government departments, members of government, members of parliament or civil servants,[1] without being able to show (in cases of libel) the truth of the

[1] Refer to article 154 of the penal code.

defamatory matter - shall be punished with imprisonment from ten days to one year.

b.2- Violence to civil servants

Violence or assault against a civil servant is punishable by the penal code. Premeditation and the intent to kill are all the more aggravated circumstances[1].

b.3- Rebellion

Any person who through violence or assault, prevents the legally authorized civil servant from performing his duty of implementing laws, rules, court decisions or lawful orders Shall also be punishable by imprisonment. Detention is substituted for imprisonment if the political nature of the infringement is established.

b.4- False statements on civil servants

In the attempt to protect the civil servant from any external constraint, the penal code hereby wants to penalize all false statements intended to influence his behaviour, notably on establishing birth, marriage or death certificates.

b.5- Constraint of civil servant

Whoever, through assault or intimidation, induces a civil servant to unduly perform an act or abstain from performing it shall be punished with a two to ten years imprisonment added with a fine from 20,000 to one million francs (article 161 of the penal code)[2].

b.6- Disturbance of services

Any one who troubles the functioning of a public service to which he does not belong is liable to be imposed six days to one month jail sentence. The civil servants so benefit from an indirect penal protection (article 185 of the penal code).

III.1.2- Guarantees on contentious issues

Contentious guarantees deal with either the recognition of a system endorsing acts of the civil servant resulting in the creation of a special

[1] Refer to article 156 of the penal code.
[2] Refer to article 161 of the penal code.

civil responsibility, or the probable recognition of a preferential jurisdiction system.

a. Civil guarantees : endorsement of the service misconduct

Cameroonian administrative case law, on the basis of usual notion of service offence, has developed a special system of civil liability, protecting permanent or temporary state workers.

In this matter the State generally endorses the misconduct of the worker, the latter engaging his own responsibility only for administrative assault (order n° 8 of october 16, 1968 affair Max Keller Ndongo versus the federated State of East Cameroon)[1]. In this case and that of expropriation, the judicial courts are competent refer exclusive to the jurisdiction of judicial courts. The State may also be share responsibilities in matter of personal offense separate from duty (order n° 8 of march 16, 1967 affair George Biau and Compagnie d'Assurances Générales versus the State of Cameroon and order Etaba Eteme and insurance company *la* Mutuelle Générale Française versus the State of Cameroon)[2].

Nevertheless the State can use legal recourse against a civil servant incriminated. The following special legal instrument, order n° 6437/CAB MFPRA of september 21, 2000 fixing the modes of legal recourse, was issued to regulate the question.

There is substitution here as of right, to the liability of the public servant condemned for personal offense against a third party.

The matter must have occurred in the course of duty or as a result from duties.

The State can then lodge a complaint against the civil servant.

The claim is materialized by issuing a recovery order to the guilty civil servant. Deductions are made on the salary of the civil servant concerned within the distrainable quota. The State can so recover the sum unduly paid to the victim. The distrainable quota shall not exceed one third of the civil servant's salary.

---

[1] See DIPANDA MOUELLE, Cour suprême du Cameroun, *Op cit.* pp. 117-118 : affair on holding his vehicle by the Administration.

[2] BINYOUM, (J.), *Les grands arrêts de la jurisprudence administrative camerounaise*, août 2008, to be published.

The minister under whom he serves is habilitated to assess the level of responsibility. He determines to this effect the corresponding share of damages to be charged, then informs the minister in charge of payments to execute the sanction.

We must keep in mind that the public agent may refer to administrative jurisdiction if he challenges the order drawn against him and claim for abuse of power.

A claim by the State does not exclude disciplinary sanctions for a personal offence.

The claim is fully justified, since the government should not be impoverished as a result of personal offences committed by its workers.

The prohibition of several proceedings for a same fact (*non ibis in dem*) cannot apply in this case as an order to pay back does not constitute an autonomous sanction.

b. Eventual existence of preferential jurisdictions

Pursuant to the French customary administrative law, civil servants carrying out high level duties enjoy the privilege of « preferential jurisdiction »[1].

In the past, article 40 of the former cameroonian public service rules and regulations provided that civil servants carrying out high-level duties did enjoy preferential jurisdiction.

This provision seems to have been removed from the general rules and regulations.

However, it may resurface in the special rules and regulations of the various corps of civil servants as determined by a decree of the president of the Republic.

Can such a particular provision prevail against non existing provisions in the general rules and regulations ?

Let us though remark that (new) article 127, of law n° 91/007 of july 30, 1991, which seemingly granted immunity to members of government clearly stipulated that any magistrate or judiciary police officer who sues, arrests or judges a member of the federal or federated governments of the

---

[1] Refer to 679 of the code of criminal procedure which provides for the possibility to chose a jurisdiction out of his area of competence.

federal or federated Assemblies, contrary to the law on immunity, is punished with a one to five years imprisonment.

III.2- THE PROTECTION OF A CIVIL SERVANT VIS-A-VIS THE STATE

Conversely, a civil servant needs protection from the State, his almighty employer. He has several guarantees at hand :

1. Workers governed by a fixed corps of rules and provisions composing the general rules and regulations of the public service on the one hand, and the particular rules, on the other hand ;

2. Jurisdictional guarantees resulting from the existing genuine case law status of the public service, forged over time through solving concrete cases by experimented magistrates initiated to administrative subtleties.

The cameroonian administrative judge started learning lessons from the French law and a proper national administrative case law has emerged on many issues of interest such as the right of defence and consultation of the disciplinary council :

- ruling n° 13 of 30 april 1963 deciding that the disciplinary council is not bound to defer on merely hearing witnesses (Nguele Jérôme versus State of Cameroon) ;

- ruling n° 1 of 4 january 1966, (State of Cameroon against Biba Théophile) rejecting the pertinent argument of introduction of fraudulent documents in the examination rooms ;

- ruling n° 4 of 22 march 1966, (Mengoumou Samuel versus the State of Cameroon) stating the inaccurate material reasons referred to, to dismiss Mr. Mengoumou of his duties as administrative assistant ;

- ruling n° 11 of 16 march 1967 (Makome spouse Albert versus the State of Cameroon) fixing the principle of communication of the file of the civil servant appearing before the disciplinary council…

3 the guarantee deriving from the right of participation and representation at the various management organs of the public service such as the higher council of the public service, the permanent disciplinary board, and health boards at all levels ;

4 guarantees inherent to the process of « jurisdictionalization » of the disciplinary procedure against civil servants becoming contradictory and in respect to the rights of defence (CFJ/CAY order n° 98 of january 27, 1970 Eteme Joseph versus Federal Republic of Cameroon) ;

5 Finally, the guarantee of an existing professional file kept by the Administration, required to contain all relevant documents as to the administrative situation and career evolution of the civil servant.

The documents must be continuously registered, numbered and classified. The professional file should not mention or indicate any political, conformist, non conformist, philosophical or religious opinion, membership to a trade union or political party. The cameroonian law does not formally authorize « professional prohibitions » for conformist or non conformist political membership, frequent in some liberal democracies. The key issue on civil servants and public liberty is therefore posed.

IV. ENJOYMENT OF PUBLIC LIBERTIES

The civil servant enjoys public liberties. As the principle is explicitly defined by public law, so are the limits, mainly as regards the right to strike.

IV.1- GRANTING PUBLIC LIBERTIES TO CIVIL SERVANTS

Article 21 of the 1994 general rules and regulations of the public service lays down : *« Civil servants shall enjoy the acknowledged rights and liberties of all citizens. They shall enjoy them within the law and regulations in force »*.

The assertion is far-reaching : the enjoyment of public liberties is acknowledged to civil servants in equal parity with common citizens.

Paragraph 2 of the same article states that they may notably be members of a legalized political or cultural association, or a professional union in view of representing or defending their professional interests.

Then further on :

« However, certain positions requiring of their incumbents loyalty to the institutions of the Republic or absolute political neutrality shall be governed by a separate enactment ».

Consideration for specific constraints of certain duties or corps has faded. The enactment on duties requiring loyalty to institutions is still awaited...

There are nevertheless several noteworthy points :

- clear principle of enjoyment of public liberties without substantial limitation ;

- authorized membership to political or cultural associations, legalized professional unions representing or defending professional interests.

Other rules furthermore reinforce this last point :

- article 22 of the general rules and regulations stipulates « *the career of a civil servant who, in a capacity other than of representative of a government service, sits in an institution set up by the law or regulations or in a body constituted to advise public authorities shall not be affected by the ideas he may express or defend therein* » ;

- article 23 declares « *a civil servant shall be entitled to the establishment of a professional file, kept by the government and containing all the documents relating to the administrative situation and the career of the civil servant. These documents shall be codified, programmed and filed on a continual basis* ».

Paragraph 2 of article 23 prescribes the following : « *Such file may not contain any mention of or document relating to the political, trade-union, philosophical or religious opinions or leanings of the civil servant concerned or his membership or non membership of a professional association or political party* ». The secular nature of the State forbids mentioning religious convictions in professional documents.

It is worth noticing recognition of a right of access to the professional file. A civil servant can request the administration to clarify, rectify, update, complete or retrieve any inaccurate, incomplete, ambiguous, out of date information, or whose collection, use, disclosure or conservation are forbidden.

The administration concerned must then effect the modification as requested, free of charge.

The burden of proof belongs to the administration towards which the right of access is exercised except if it has been proven that the contested information was provided and approved by the civil servant concerned.

The civil servant enjoys public freedoms.

However he is bound to "*to exercise his rights with all due respect for the authority of the State and for law and order*" (article 21, paragraph 3).

In the past, the rules underlined ethical requirements other than the authority of the State, especially certain constraints specific to certain functions.

IV.2- LIMITATION OF PUBLIC LIBERTY

Certain limitations are expressly posed by the rules and regulations while others may be implicit.

IV.2.1- Statutory limitations

There is a difference between express and implicit limitations.

a. Express limitations

The 1994 rules and regulations resumed article 45 of the former rules in article 40, paragraph 1 : « *a civil servant shall be bound by the obligation of reserve in the discharge of his duties* ».

Further on, it states : « *the obligation of reserve shall consist in abstaining from publicly proclaiming his political, philosophical, religious or trade union opinions and in not performing service on the basis of the said opinions* ».

The new text clarified the position a great deal : the prohibition seems to relate to public expression of opinions. Where shall we draw the line between private and public as regards the obligation of reserve ?

The obligation of reserve traditionally requires, while on duty a minimum of loyalty and off duty the obligation for the civil servant not to express his opinions in a rude or insulting manner against public powers or his superiors.

b. Implicit limitations

In the past, high-ranking officials (article 16 of the former rules and regulations) whose list was discretionary enjoyed less public freedoms than any other.

It is even reasonable to assert that they had a very tight margin to act. In fact no State in the world would stand being criticized by its divisional officers or ambassadors.

High level duties are not mentioned any more in the new rules. A new similar category, whose list will be determined by a special enactment, has come out « *positions requiring of their incumbents loyalty to the institutions of the Republic or absolute political neutrality* » (article 21, last paragraph).

IV.2.2- Limitations deduced from general or special enactments

The regulations of certain corps in particular restrict public freedoms yet recognized to the members : military personnel, policemen, penitentiary administration…

That is why the special status of these "special corps" reinforce their disciplinary dispositions.

Decree n° 74/250 of 4th April fixing the special regulations of the corps of civil servants of the penitentiary administration declares disciplinary sanctions applicable similar to those applicable to officers and soldiers, and any breach of duty and actions disturbing public order are considered as disciplinary misconducts.

The special regulations of civil servants of the national security are very clear, as civil servants of this corps shall at any time abstain in public from making any gesture, speaking any word or demonstration susceptible to discredit national institutions, the corps to which they belong, or trouble the public order. He is not authorized to strike [1].

A French law of 30 august 1883 forbids magistrates to demonstrate against the Republic.

IV.3- THE RIGHT TO STRIKE

Whether it is appropriate or not, the debate remains open. The history of the right to strike tells how difficult the transition from illegality to legality was, and the study of cameroonian positive law in this regard points out the absence of precise regulations.

---

[1] Refer to decree n° 77/48 of february 14, 1977 fixing the special status of national security and subsequent texts

IV.3.1- Debate after granting the right to strike

Opponents to this right enumerate the following arguments to deny the right to strike to that particular category of citizens : civil servants ;

- the right to strike contradicts the fundamental principle of continuity in the public service that shall operate without interruption ;

- it is a crime against the authority in flagrant contradiction with the spirit of hierarchical subordination inherent to the public service.

How could the administration, which unilaterally decides the working conditions of civil servants via administrative acts with automatic execution, tolerate that civil servants question again these conditions by striking ?

It would be only fair to limit or cancel the right of strike in return to privileges civil servants do enjoy.

A strike initiated by civil servants would signify rebellion, anti-development, a subversive act of utmost seriousness.

Yet supporters of the right to strike are not at all impressed by the above arguments :

- to them, the right to strike would be the main tool for the freedom of association guaranteed to all workers and even civil servants.

- There should be no legal reason to make systematic discrimination between private employees and State workers a basic rule, putting at stake the general rule of all citizens equal before the law.

Nothing *a priori* justifies in any case qualifying strikes in public services as utmost serious, insofar as certain strikes of the private sector equally severely undermine the general interest of citizens (for instance the bakers' strike), etc.

IV.3.2- History : from illegality to legality

From the recent history of the French administrative law, by reference to our own, a clear break was marked in 1946 in the idea of the right of civil servants to strike.

a. Illegality of the right to strike before 1946

Before 1946, strike was illegal in the French public service and considered as a disciplinary offence, resulting without warranty, to sanctions for the civil servants involved. It was a breach of contract by the civil servant himself who deliberately put himself out of the protective statutory guarantees of the public service.

The State endeavoured to fight against strikes by resorting to staff requisition (law of july 1938) and the call to reservists.

b. Legality of the right to strike after 1946 in the public service

In the preamble of the French Constitution of 1946 it was stated that the right to strike was exercised within the law governing it. The 1946 General Rules did not mention anything on the matter, nor laid down any regulation. The legal problem posed was elusive : did the right to strike recognized by the Constitution remain forbidden to civil servants, or did it have to wait, for a special enactment defining the modes of strikes within the public service before implementation ?

The State council was going to give a decision by recognizing the right to strike to civil servants (7 luly1950, order Dehaene). The case law solution remained tenuous in the absence of appropriate rules.

IV.3.3- Absence of cameroonian regulations

The general rules and regulations acknowledge the legality of eventual legalized associations of civil servants to present and defend professional interests.

There is no provision in positive law ruling any potential recourse to strike for these organizations. The French system may serve as reference.

On the one hand, the law of july, 31,•1963, codified the right of civil servants to strike in France. The strike was to be obligatorily preceded by a written notice indicating the time, place and date of the demonstration.

« Outflanking strikes » are banned in administrations. Failing to observe these rules, an expeditious disciplinary procedure is started that does not include the communication of the file, for sanctions below dismissal and demotion in rank or class. Strike, by virtue of the principle of remuneration after service done, entails a deduction in salary at least equal to one day salary.

On the other hand, special provisions limit or exclude the right to strike of certain categories of civil servants : republican security divisions (law of december, 17, 1974), national police (law of september 28, 1948), penitentiary administration (law of august 5, 1958), magistracy (ordinance of december, 22, 1958), air traffic controllers and air safety electronic engineers (1[str] july 1964).

Cameroonian public law, law of development, cannot but accentuate some restrictive tendencies of civil servants right to strike. Strike is explicitly forbidden to state workers of the cameroonian national Security (refers to special rules, decree n° 77/48 of february, 14, 1977).

CONCLUSION

The public service law in Cameroon even though inspired by its French counterpart, progressively differs from it, especially through the primacy of ruling sources, a sign of the Cameroonian constitutional presidential system. This renders the status of these rules somehow precarious.

APPENDIXES

APPENDIX 1 :
DATA ON CAMEROON STATE EMPLOYEES

Appendix 1.1 : Distribution by corps and category of state employees on duty as at December 31, 1982

CATEGORIES CORPS		NUMBER OF CIVIL SERVANTS							
		A2	A1	B2	B1	C	D	TOTAL	%
General Administration		79	416	77	478	1 806	2 006	4 862	12,09
School and Univ. Administration		-	17	8	15	-	-	40	0,1
Health Administration		1	20	2	16	-	-	39	0,1
Diplomacy		37	76	-	-	-	-	113	0,28
Court Registry		-	26	55	129	346	738	1 294	3,33
Labour and Social Security		10	57	14	69	112	134	396	0,99
Translation and Interpretation		28	3	-	-	-	-	31	0,08
Customs (active corps)		-	14	5	34	135	442	630	1,57
Financial Administrations	Treasury	16	116	19	106	207	286	750	1,87
	Taxation	7	75	3	99	69	83	336	0,84
	Stamp duty	3	20	4	24	37	82	170	0,42
	Customs	12	55	14	38	175	165	459	1,14
Stores accounting		-	11	-	42	79	72	204	0,51
Information		22	141	30	27	66	31	317	0,79
Industrial Techniques		5	1	8	10	6	50	80	0,2
Civil Engineering		51	68	168	68	227	176	758	1,89
Mines and Geology		61	8	-	12	11	15	107	0,27
Surveys		16	16	93	51	139	89	404	1
Geographical Service		3	3	1	2	9	8	26	0,06
Statistics		36	89	18	108	107	18	376	0,94
Demography		19	-	-	-	-	-	19	0,05
Information		15	22	7	26	22	10	102	0,25
Exploitation of P and T		37	98	42	300	923	766	2 166	5,39
Telecommunications Techniques		14	34	23	56	67	28	222	0,55
Livestock and Sea Fishing		42	7	16	136	296	92	582	1,47
Animal Industries		2	1	1	-	1	44	49	0,12
Agriculture		250	237	22	611	710	273	2103	5,23
Waters and Forestry		35	22	8	148	138	173	524	1,3
Rural Engineering		34	6	65	39	48	16	208	0,52
Meteorology		11	14	8	31	68	98	230	0,57
Civil Aeronautics		17	6	26	67	92	5	213	0,53

National Printing Press	-	-	6	7	27	10	50	0,12
Higher Education	151	-	-	-	-	-	151	0,37
General Education	798	1 713	180	3 045	5 944	1 663	13 343	33,19
Technical Education	18	93	66	345	381	23	926	2,3
Youth and Sports	28	39	13	354	39	16	489	1,22
Youth and Community-based Activities	54	2	4	65	12	-	137	0,34
Sports and Physical Education	100	2	18	126	143	11	400	0,99
Public Health	383	69	123	1 129	1 817	3 029	6 550	16,29
Social Affairs	3	7	35	130	144	18	337	0,84
Whole	2 398	3 604	1 182	7 943	14 443	10 670	40 200	100
% By categories	5,96	8,97	2,94	19,76	35,83	26,54	-	-

Source : Workforce Control Department, Public Service.

Appendix 1.2 : Distribution by province of origin and category of contract staff of the Cameroonian administration

CATEGORY PROVINCE	**NUMBER OF CONTRACT WORKERS**										**%**
	5	**6**	**7**	**8**	**9**	**10**	**11**	**12**	**INDET***	**TOTAL**	
CENTRE-SOUTH	18	97	1 081	1 346	143	187	19	2	72	2 965	38,48
EAST	2	7	63	57	6	12	2	-	4	153	1,98
WEST	8	36	460	977	94	128	24	-	49	1 776	23,05
NORTH	2	1	35	57	3	9	1	-	8	116	1,5
LITORAL	3	39	330	505	59	158	26	-	62	1 180	15,31
NORTH-WEST	5	1	348	326	35	34	3	-	26	778 541	10,1
SOUTH-WEST	-	-	202	247	23	52	1	1	15	194	7,02
Born abroad	-	5	19	36	14	48	10	-	60	1	-
Unspecified	-	-	-	1	-	-	-	-	-		0,01
TOTAL	38	186	2538	3 552	377	628	86	3	296	7 704	-
% PER CATEGORY	0,49	2,42	32,94	46,11	4,89	8,15	1,12	0,04	3,84	-	100

Source : Public Service. Workforce Control Department, Bureau of Statistics.

*They are contractual agents with a global or indexed salary.

Appendix 1.3 : Distribution by category and user department of government contract employees recruited within the period January 1 to December 31, 1982.

DEPARTMENTS CATEGORIES USERS	NUMBER OF CONTRACTUALS									TOTAL	%
	5	6	7	8	9	10	11	12	IND		
Presidency	-	-	6	10	2	1	-	-	1	20	2,2
Ministry Del.Insp. General of the	-	-	1	2	-	-	-	-	-	3	0,3
State	-	-	1	1	-	-	-	-	-	2	0,2
Mini Del. In Ch. of Rel. with	-	-	3	3	-	5	-	-	-	11	1,2
Parliament	-	-	12	5	1	2	-	-	-	20	2,2
Services of the Prime Ministry	-	-	3	5	-	1	-	-	9	1,0	
Ministry of Territorial Administration	-	-	3	3	1	4	2	1	1	15	1,6
Ministry of Foreign Affairs	-	-	5	9	1	2	-	-	-	17	1,7
Ministry of Social Affairs.	-	-	23	15	-	22	1	-	-	61	6,6
Ministry of Agriculture	-	-	67	228	5	12	-	-	313	34,2	
Ministry of Economy and Planning	-	-	3	2	-	-	-	-	-	5	0,5
Ministry of National Education	-	-	9	6	-	4	-	-	-	19	2,1
Min. of Livestock and Animal	-	-	58	48	2	16	-	-	-	124	13,5
Breeding	-	-	4	4	-	2	-	-	1	11	1,2
Ministry of Equipment	-	-	3	6	-	-	-	-	-	9	1,0
Ministry of Finance	-	-	9	18	5	12	-	-	-	44	4,8
Ministry of Public Service	-	-	5	4	-	-	-	-	-	10	1,1
Ministry of Armed Forces	-	-	5	6	1	5	-	-	-	17	1,9
Ministry of Information and Culture	-	-	2	1	1	-	-	-	5	0,5	
Ministry of Youth and Sports	-	-	1	3	-	12	-	-	-	16	1,7
Ministry of Post and Telecom.	-	-	16	14	4	4	3	-	-	41	4,5
Ministry of Justice	-	-	5	5	-	7	-	-	-	17	1,9
Ministry of Mines and Power	-	-	7	4	1	2	-	-	-	14	1,5
Ministry of Public Health	-	-	5	2	-	-	-	-	-	7	0,8
Ministry of Transport	-	-	4	6	-	2	-	-	-	12	1,3
Min. of Labour and Social Insurance	-	-	11	6	3	9	1	-	64	94	10,3
General Delegation for Tourism											
Urbanism and Housing											
D.G.R.S.T.											
WHOLE	-	-	271	416	27	125	8	2	67	916	100,0

Source : Workforce Control Department, Public Service.

Appendix 1.4 : Distribution of Staff of State personnel, by corps in 2008

CORPS	**PERSONNEL**
General administration	2 552
School and university administration	26
Civil aeronautics	8
Social affairs	523
Agriculture	3 457
Cadastre	358
Dental surgeon	30
School and university career adviser	180
Contractuals	26 773
Decision makers	8 808
Demographs	74
Diplomacy	191
Documentation	421
Active customs	1 039
Water and forestry	927
Physical and sports education	2 066
Livestock and fishing	933
General education	23 837
Primary and nursery education	26 541
Higher education	1 686
Technical education	6 087
Civil engineering	1 069
Rural engeneering	384
Sanitary engeneering	452
Nurses	5 722
Computer scientists	81
Information	453
Animal industries	288
Youth and animation	956
Youth and sport	5
Medecine	1 758
Meteorology	62
Mines and geology	76
Chemist	74
Post	1 130
Prices, weights and measures	36
Financial boards (customs)	589
Financial boards (registrations)	119
Financial boards (taxes)	1 206
Financial boards (treasury)	1 11
Geographical services	11

Statistics	569
Medico-sanitary technicians	1 045
Industrial techniques	104
Telecommunications	695
Labour and social insurance	247
Translators interpreters	101
TOTAL	**126 482**

APPENDIX 2 :
THE MAILLET SCALE OF DISABILITY ASSESSMENT

Sources : Directorate of legal and administrative information French Documentation

Appendix 2.1 : Calculation of pension for industrial accidents

Revaluated minimum pension rate as at 1st of April 2011 for minimum old age and pension fund, 03, 31 2011

The ministers of Economy and Labour announced 2,1% and 4,7% upgrading of the retirement pension and the minimum pension rate respectively, as from 1st April 2011.

These revalorization coefficients are applied to other benefits, in particular disability pensions and pensions for industrial accidents.

These annual increases have not yet been passed into law.

Information contained in the present page is currently being actualized before enactment.

a. Method of Calculation :

The calculation of the pension granted to the victims with a degree of disability equal to or above 10% is based on the 12 calendar months preceding the cessation of work.

Remark : in some cases provided under the social insurance code, the annual salary can be partly reconstituted, for example, when the period considered includes periods of unemployment or cessation of work due to illness.

b. Determination of the basic salary

The annual salary is totally taken into account for the calculation of pension, if it doesn't go beyond ceiling of 34,384€, equivalent to twofold the minimum salary for pension incomes whose amount, since April 2010, has been fixed at 17,192€.

When the annual salary is more than the ceiling, then only one third of the fraction of remuneration comprised between 34,384€ and 137,536€ shall be considered in the calculation of the pension. When the annual salary is above 137,536€, the fraction of the remuneration exceeding this amount is not taken into account for the calculation of the pension.

Pension cannot be calculated for an annual salary that is less than a 17,192€ (amounts in force as of first April 2010).

c. Calculation of pension from the rate of disability

The amount of the pension corresponds to a percentage of the annual salary considered. It consists of :

- half the permanent disability rate (IP) granted by the health insurance primary fund (CPAM) when the rate is below or equal to 50% ;

- one and a half the IP rate above 50%.

Examples :

- for a person with a 30% degree of disability recognized by the CPAM, the rate used to calculate the pension will be 15% (30 :2 = 15% x annual salary),

- for a person with an acknowledged 75% disability, the rate applied on the annual salary to calculate the pension will be 62.5% (50 :2=25%) + (25x1.5=37.5%) = 62.5% x annual salary).

d. Incremental pension for a third party (Amount in force on the 1st of April 2010)

If the degree of disability approved by the health insurance is equal to or above 80%, and if the victim is forced, due to his disability, to resort to assistance from third party, the amount of the pension is increased by 40%.

Such an amount shall not be less than 1.038,36€ per month.

e. Party revalorisation

Since 2009, the revalorization coefficient is revised every year on 1st of April. In 2010, the pensions were increased by 0,9%.

Appendix 2.2 : Granting a pension or a capital allowance

a. Principle

Any person who suffers from a permanent disability resulting from an industrial accident or an occupational illness is entitled to receive :

- either a capital allowance, if his permanent disability is under 10% ;

- or a pension for permanent disability equal or above 10% ;

- Capital allowance is a lump sum whose amount varies proportionally with the degree of disability ;

- the permanent disability pension, given periodically, is determined both by the degree of disability and the salaries of the last 12 months preceding the cessation of work due to an industrial accident or a professional illness.

b. Degree of disability

Determination

It is fixed by the Health Insurance Fund, depending on medical and professional criteria and from an indicative scale of disability, after the medical consultant's advice.

The victim or his beneficiaries are informed of the decision by written notice, and have ten days within which to apply for a copy of the medical report by filling in a form appended to the notice.

In the case of consecutive accidents.

Before the 1st of January 2000, each accident was treated individually. For accidents reported since that date :

- the degrees of disability previously approved are taken into account to calculate the pension of the latest accident, whose rates give right a pension or capital allowance ;

- degrees of disability below 10% may be cumulated to benefit from a pension when the drawing of more than one salary makes the 10% minimal rate.

Remark : these amendments also apply for accidents or occupational diseases that were previously reported, when a change was observed in the health state of the victim from 1srt of january 2000, resulting in an additional compensation.

c. The right to choose between capital allowance and pension scheme

Principle

In case of consecutive accidents resulting in a disability evaluated below 10%, thus giving right to several capital allowances, the addition of these degrees of disability may entitle to a pension, if the sum is equal to or over 10%.

The victim may thus select one option between receiving a lump sum for capital allowance for the last accident, or an "optional" pension whose calculation is based on the addition of the successive accidents recorded.

Notification of the decision informing of the right notice to option

After all conditions are fulfilled, the health insurance fund must inform the victim by recommended mail with acknowledgement of receipt, of his right to choose an option. The notice must include the following details :

- degree of permanent disability and corresponding capital amount ;

- option between capital allowance and annuities, mentioning the rate and amount ;

- two month to challenge the degree of disability ;

- two month to opt for annuities ;

- failing to answer within two months entails the payment of a capital allowance.

Consequences

The option for annuities is irrevocable.

The interested party cannot surrender the annuities.

The optional annuity cannot moreover be paid to the surviving spouse.

Deduction of a fraction of capital allowances on the first "optional" payments of annuities.

On paying the optional annuities, part of the capital allowances (IC) are deducted from the annual pension amount, up to half the IC already paid.

The deduction is further spread on the first annuities, considering the 30% annual ceiling of deductions. This results in a reduction of the first installment.

Appendix 2.3 : Amount of Capital allowance paid to the victim of an industrial accident

Upgrading as of 1rst of April 2011 of the minimum old age allowance and old age pension annuities-31.3.2011.

The ministers of the Economy and Labour announced the 2,1% and 4,7% upgrading of the retirement pension and the minimal pension rate respectively, as from 1st April 2011.

These upgraded coefficients are applied to other benefits, in particular invalidity pensions and pensions for industrial accidents.

These annual increases have not yet been passed into law.

Information contained in the present page is currently being actualized before the awaited enactment.

Amount of the capital allowance upgraded as of first April 2010

Table relating to file F 14854

Degree of Permanent Disability	Amount of capital allowance
1%	388,56€
2%	631,53€
3%	922,85€
4%	1.456,54€
5%	1.845,14€
6%	2.282,13€
7%	2.767,47€
8%	3.301,76€
9%	3.884,38€

Appendix 2.4 : Revision of the calculation of the industrial accident pension

a. Principle

The annuity may be revised in case of health improvement or healing of the concerned. If the health insurance fund observes, on request of the beneficiary or after a control by medical services, that the disability rate has changed, a revision procedure is set in motion.

When the degree of disability goes below the 10% threshold, the revision may have as effect to keep the same level of annuities, change its rate, or convert the annuity into a capital allowance.

b. Who may request the revision ?

The revision may be made on the initiative of :

- the health insurance primary fund. After healing or mending, the health insurance fund may actually require the victim of an industrial accident to perform medical control tests. They may take place quarterly during the first two years, then once a year thereafter.

- the victim of the accident ;

- the nominated beneficiaries, in the event of death caused by the accident.

c. Delays

The application for revision must be made only after the healing or mending of the condition of the victim. It must be linked to deterioration in health or recovery after a stable health condition.

It may be requested at any time during the 2 years following the healing or recovery. After two years, the revision can be requested only once a year, unless the victim and the insurance health fund agree to do it.

d. Procedure

The request must be submitted to the health insurance fund in charge of paying the annuities or capital allowance by registered mail, or on the spot, in writing, and include all written evidence of the health progress.

Appendix 2.5 : Annuities for the beneficiaries of victims of industrial accidents

a. Beneficiaries

In case the accident or illness caused the death of the victim, his beneficiaries may be granted annuities. Those concerned are :

-the spouse, common law husband/wife, or partner under PACS (civil solidarity pact) ;

- children ;

- ascendants.

b. Surviving spouse

The survivorship annuity is up to 40% of the basic annual salary of the victim under certain conditions :

- they were married before the occurrence of the accident ;
- they were married at least two years before the death of the insured ;
- one or more children were born from the union.

c. Increment for the disability stricken spouse

When the survivor is 55 years old, or if before this age, he/she became stricken with a minimum industrial disability of 50% for 3 months, an increase in the life annuity equal to 20% of the basic annual salary of the victim is also due.

In the second case (a spouse with industrial disability) the increase is paid as long as the disability is established.

The request must be made on a Cerfa n°6001-3555 form, to which a medical certificate is appended.

d. Separated or divorced former spouse

The divorced or separated spouses who had obtained alimony before the death of the victim, may benefit from annuities equal to the amount of the alimony, not exceeding 20% of the basic annual salary of the victim.

e. Remarriage

If the victim had married again before his death, the life annuity to be granted to his new surviving spouse is at least equivalent to 20% of the basic annual salary of the insured ;

When the surviving spouse marries again, he/she is no more entitled to survivorship annuity. Instead, a capital amount is paid to him/her, threefold the annual total amount of the annuity he used to receive.

However, as long as the children beneficiaries get themselves an annuity, the former spouse who remarried still keeps his/her right to annuities.

f. Common law husband /wife or partner under PACS

For accidents having occurred before the 1st of September 2001, Common law husband /wife and PACS partners may also be granted an annuity equal to 40% of the basic annual salary of the victim. The conditions are similar to those of marriage :

- PACS partners must have signed the pact, or the cohabitation must have been established before the date of the accident ;

- or instead, at least 2 years as of the date of death of the insured ;

- or the couple has one or more children.

g. Children

Orphans benefit from a beneficiary annuity until age 20, computed on the basis of a percentage of the annual salary of the victim, from 20% to 30%, according to the number of children and whether the second parent is living or not.

Ascendants

If they can prove that :

- the victim had no spouse or child able to henceforth qualify for the obligation of alimony ;

- or they were already dependent on the victim when he died (in this case, the existence of a spouse or children does not hinder the payment of annuities), and they may receive an annuity corresponding to 10% of the annual salary, limited to 30% for all the ascendants.

If in excess of this last percentage, the annuity is proportionally reduced for each ascendant.

Appendix 2.6 : Capital allowance and industrial accident annuity payment and scheme

a. Payment of the capital allowance

The capital allowance is a lump sum paid once.

b. Payment of annuities

Permanent disability annuity is a life annuity paid out until the death of the annuitant.

It can be paid quarterly or monthly when the disability rate is up to 50%.

The beneficiaries' annuity is paid on a quarterly base.

c. Tax scheme for capital allowance and annuities

Both capital allowance and annuities are exempted from the general social contribution (CSG) and contribution to the reimbursement of the social debt (CRDS).

They are income tax free.

d. Possible cumulated pensions

Pensions allocated by the health insurance to compensate for industrial accidents or occupational illnesses may be cumulated with disability or retirement pensions.

However the above is restricted when the disability pension was awarded in the case of infirmities or illnesses resulting from the accident that led to the payment of the annuity.

Social system appropriate to serious disability

If the permanent disability is equal to or above 66,66%, the victim and his beneficiaries, except for drugs bearing a blue label which are partially reimbursed (35%), have their medical care and treatment totally paid for (100%).

BIBLIOGRAPHY

I. BOOKS AND COLLECTION OF COURT RULINGS

- AUBY, J. M. et DUCOS-ADER, R. (1973) : *Droit administratif. La Fonction publique.* Paris, Dalloz.

- BINYOUM, J. : *Recueil des grands arrêts de la jurisprudence administrative camerounaise.* (to be published).

- GAZIER, F. : *La fonction publique dans le monde*, Paris, Edition Cujas, Bibliothèque de L'IIAP, 246 pages.

- OWONA, J. (1985) : *Droit Administratif spécial de la République du Cameroun*, EDICEF, Série Manuels et Travaux de l'Université de Yaoundé.

- TEKAM, G. J. (2006) : *Fonction publique camerounaise Statut Général et textes d'application, recueil des textes commentés.*

- TEKAM, G. J. (2010) : *Déontologie et éthique professionnelle du fonctionnaire*, Yaoundé, Éditions SOPECAM.

II. REGULATORY INSTRUMENTS, LAWS AND CODES

- Code du travail camerounais annoté. Collection Textes usuels, Presses Universitaires d'Afrique, 1997.

- Code des lois pénales de la République du Cameroun, Collection Textes usuels, Presses Universitaires d'Afrique, 1998.

- (New) Criminal Procedure Code. Collection Textes usuels, Presses Universitaires d'Afrique, édition bilingue, mars 2006.

- Decree n° 74/138 of 18 february 1974 to lay down rules and regulations of the Public Service and subsequent amendments

Statut général de la Fonction publique et les textes qui le modifient (JORUC n° 1(supplément) du 15/08/1974).

- Decree n°78/484 of 9 November 1978 to lay down common rules to apply to State agents governed by the Labour Code (JORUC n°22 of 11/15/1978, p. 2232).

- Decree n° 94/199 of 7 october 1994 on the General Rules and Regulations of the Public Service amended and completed by Decree 200/287 of 12 October 2000.

-Decree n° 74/759 of 26 august 1974 to organize civil pension schemes and subsequent amendments there.

- Decree n° 78/488 of 9 november 1978 defining the attribution of civil and military pensions, life annuities, capital and death allowances.

- Law n°2004/17 of 22 july 2004 on the orientation of decentralization.

- Loi n°2004/18 of 22 july 2004 to lay down rules applicable to councils.

- Law n°2004/19 of july to lay down rules applicable to regions 2004.

III. COURT RULINGS

- DIPANDA MOUELLE, A. : *Grands arrêts de la jurisprudence Administrative de la Cour Fédérale de Justice*, Ministère de la justice, deux tomes, années 1967 et 1970, et 1970-1975, Première édition, Imprimerie nationale.

- DIPANDA MOUELLE, A. : *Droit Administratif. Répertoire chronologique de la jurisprudence de la Cour suprême du Cameroun*, Première partie, Tome V, année 1960-1980, Première édition, Imprimerie nationale.

CONTENTS

L'HARMATTAN ITALIE
Via Degli Artisti 15; 10124 Torino

L'HARMATTAN HONGRIE
Könyvesbolt ; Kossuth L. u. 14-16
1053 Budapest

L'HARMATTAN BURKINA FASO
Rue 15.167 Route du Pô Patte d'oie
12 BP 226 Ouagadougou 12
(00226) 76 59 79 86

ESPACE L'HARMATTAN KINSHASA
Faculté des Sciences sociales,
politiques et administratives
Université de Kinshasa
BP243, KIN XI

L'HARMATTAN CONGO
67, av. E. P. Lumumba
Bât. – Congo Pharmacie (Bib. Nat.)
BP2874 Brazzaville
harmattan.congo@yahoo.fr

L'HARMATTAN GUINÉE
Almamya Rue KA 028, en face du restaurant Le Cèdre
OKB agency BP 3470 Conakry
(00224) 60 20 85 08
harmattanguinee@yahoo.fr

L'HARMATTAN CÔTE D'IVOIRE
M. Etien N'dah Ahmon
Résidence Karl / cité des arts
Abidjan-Cocody 03 BP 1588 Abidjan 03
(00225) 05 77 87 31

L'HARMATTAN MAURITANIE
Espace El Kettab du livre francophone
N° 472 avenue du Palais des Congrès
BP 316 Nouakchott
(00222) 63 25 980

L'HARMATTAN CAMEROUN
BP 11486
Face à la SNI, immeuble Don Bosco
Yaoundé
(00237) 99 76 61 66
harmattancam@yahoo.fr

L'HARMATTAN SÉNÉGAL
« Villa Rose », rue de Diourbel X G, Point E
BP 45034 Dakar FANN
(00221) 33 825 98 58 / 77 242 25 08
senharmattan@gmail.com

535935 - Juillet 2013
Achevé d'imprimer par
1livre.com
du rêve à la réalité !

Made in United States
Orlando, FL
04 November 2026

90200856R00142